Better Known as
JOHNNY
APPLESEED

BETTER KNOWN AS

JOHNNY APPLE-SEED

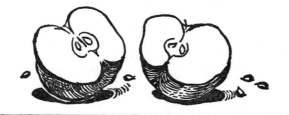

BY MABEL LEIGH HUNT

Decorations by James Daugherty

J. B. LIPPINCOTT COMPANY
PHILADELPHIA & NEW YORK

Fifteenth Printing

ISBN-0-397-30163-4

*This book is
Designed by Helen Gentry
Set in Janson 11/15 type and printed by*
VAIL-BALLOU PRESS, INC.,
BINGHAMTON, N. Y.

Library of Congress Catalog Card Number 50-14382

TO MY SISTERS

Helen Hunt Oberreich

AND

Agnes Hunt Calvert

AND

TO THE MEMORY

OF ANOTHER

Carrie Hunt Latta

FOREWORD

IN THE RICH beautiful country of Ohio and Indiana there has been slowly growing for more than a century a legend not very different from that of St. Francis of Assisi. It concerns a humble man regarded in his day as an eccentric but a man who was universally loved in the frontier wilderness country by Indians and white settlers alike. His needs were simple and his affection for man, for the animals and birds, for the trees and wildflowers was very great. He was, perhaps as much as any man has ever been, a very part of this natural world in which we live and from which many of us, to our great loss, today live divorced and isolated.

For those of us who live in the beautiful rich country where Johnny Appleseed lived and worked for the good and peace of mankind, he is a real and living legend which each year grows a little as folk tales grow. He still moves about among us through the beautiful hardwood forests and marshes which in summer take on the luxuriance of the tropics. We know him when we pass the wild apple trees in the tangled fence rows and the pink-flowering, richly perfumed wild crabs which are related to those first trees which he planted in the Western country. When our feet trample the wild fennel and the aromatic scent reaches our nostrils we think of Johnny Appleseed who first brought it into the frontier country as a specific against "fever and ague." When the spring burgeons and the delicate and delicious morels appear among the trilliums and Dutchman's breeches and wild violets, you have the feeling that somewhere nearby among the trees of the thick forest the ghost of Johnny Appleseed is watching you. He is in our lives, in the memory of the tales told of him by our grandparents and great-grandparents.

Mabel Leigh Hunt, Midwestern writer of Johnny Appleseed's own country, studied his life, absorbed his character, loved and collected his legends for years, in preparation for writing her book. It is both important and charming. If you live outside the area in which he lived and roamed you will come, through its pages, to know him as we in Ohio and Indiana know him.

Louis Bromfield
Malabar Farm

PREFACE

THE PANORAMA of Johnny Appleseed's life and legend is like a delicate old tapestry, its fabric worn with age and much handling, its fabulous leaves and flowers and fruits, its beasts and men ofttimes undiscernible, its fantastic story not quite clear. It is rich and humorous and lovely. It could never be anything but American.

"But was Johnny Appleseed a real person?" Most assuredly, yes. Through the contrivance of both fiction and biographical narrative I have attempted, in this book, to present the real man as he has appeared to me. All of the existent documents and historical evidences relating to him are known to me through close and extensive research. But since I had no inclination to write a documentary book, I have made use of but portions of such material, enough, I hope, to prove to readers the reality of John Chapman, and to show the main outlines of his life and travels.

But a book about Johnny Appleseed would lack savor, sentiment and richness unless use is also made of the many legends which cluster about his name. In general, those which I have recounted are based upon personal reminiscences found in old county histories, and enlarged, perhaps, through the processes of time and repetition. Yet the narrators who described Johnny Appleseed's person and activities agreed on salient points to a remarkable degree; although they lived in widely scattered localities, and transmitted their stories long, long before there was a revival of public interest in him. It must be remembered that Johnny was legendary in the minds of men while he still moved among them. From the beginning they gave him his delightful nickname—*Appleseed John* when first they noticed him; *Johnny Appleseed* when they learned to love him. Life and legend are one and the same, inseparably fused. But this is, as near as I could make it by the methods chosen, an account of the *founding* of that legend.

Dates are approximate only. They overlap because the three divisions of the book necessarily overlap in time and circumstance. It was impossible to introduce all the localities frequented by Johnny. Because a creative writer must contrive, I have allowed him to talk of himself, although in the same breath I have said he did little of it.

Mabel Leigh Hunt
Indianapolis, Indiana
January, 1950

CONTENTS

xii   CONTENTS

Michigan

Goshen

St. Joseph River

Fort Defiance 1828

Fort Wayne 1828
Mar. 18, 1845

Maumee

Hancock Co.

St. Marys River

Wabash River

St. Marys
Mercer Co.

Auglaize Co.

← To Missouri 1843
and Iowa, probably
following watercourses

Fort Recovery

Logan Co.

Greenville

1836
Urbana
Champaign

N
W — E
S

Richmond

Clark Co.

Old Town

Legend

Buffalo & Indian Trail ·······
Indian Towns ⚑
J.A.'s nurseries
and dates 🌳
J.A.'s cabins 🏠
Memorials ✳

Indiana

Oxford

The Gore

Treaty Line 1795

Fort Hamilton

Miami Purchase

1826
Cincinnati
Fort Washington

Virginia Military Lands

500 miles

The Mississippi River

Kentucky

River

Iroquois War Path

F. Murdoch

Lake Erie

Great Iroquois Trail

Cleveland

Western Reserve
(to Connecticut)

Sandusky

FIRE LANDS
Huron Co.
1811

Pennsylvania

Fort Duquesne Pittsburgh

Ashland
Ashland Co.

Fort Laurens

Mansfield
Richland Co.
1814

Seven Ranges

Mt Vernon
Knox Co.

Cos-hoc-Ton
Tuscarawas

Steubenville
Jefferson Co.
1806

Newark

Licking

Zane's Trace
old Buffalo Trail
Baxter City

Wheeling
To Romes R.

Road

National Trail
East 1800

Zanesville

Ohio Company

Olentangy Trail

Chillicothe

Chapman home 1805

Marietta

Blennerhassett Island

Virginia

Kanawha River
to LaSalle 1670

"Johnny Appleseed"
his Map
of the Ohio Country
Compiled & sketched
by friends
1945

Courtesy of the Swedenborg Press

Mr Martin Mason Sir please
to let Elder Mire or bearer have
thirty-Eight apple trees and you will
Oblige your friend
Richland Co Ohio   John Chapman
August the 21st 1818

FACSIMILE OF AN ORDER BY JOHNNY APPLESEED

Part I
THE SEEDS

I. THE MORNING LIGHT

SOME villages cannot boast of a single brook to brighten their lanes and byways with its sparkle and music. Not even in the old days, when abundant-flowing water was far more common than now. But down from the twelve hills overlooking the village of Leominster in Massachusetts Bay Colony, and from the mother ponds which spread their sheeted waters in the outlying meadows, tumbled several swift, silvery currents. Eventually they lost themselves in the Nashua River that wound through the town, but while they ran free, the brooks of Leominster took their own merry will and pleasure.

Everyone knows that a brook is talkative water. It gossips continually and very prettily. And on a Monday in apple-cider time, on September 26th, 1774, to be exact, perhaps it was only Leominster's brooks that chattered of the birth of a new baby, for among the big families of the colonies, babies were not unusual.

This particular new arrival added but one more to Leominster's nine-hundred-and-some inhabitants, none

3

of whom, it is quite certain, knew how to translate the
fluid language of brooks. Even had it suddenly become
plain to them, they would have called it blather, and
thought themselves gone foolish, or that some outlandish
devilry was in the air. They would have kept it to themselves, scurrying off in embarrassment and alarm, each to
his own business, whether it was tanning hides or fulling
cloth, grinding meal or gathering the autumn harvest of
grains and fruits.

"Stupid ones with the big dull ears," mocked the brooks,
tumbling with laughter, "in the Chapman house by the
river is a newborn child who shall become one of America's best-loved legends. Hearken, you minister and law-
yer, you innholder and deacon! Long after your pompous
selves are forgotten, this humble child shall live on in song
and story. And you lesser folk, who this September day
press your rosy apples into cider, or string your dried-
apple slices for winter pies—little do you dream that the
name of *Johnny Appleseed* shall grace a thousand apple
festivals, and he himself be acclaimed the patron saint of
fruiting orchards!"

The chatter of the brooks meant nothing to Nathanael
and Elizabeth Chapman either. They saw naught that was
extraordinary about their new baby. Oh, they were proud
of him, of course, for they were young and in love, and
this their first son, brother to their four-year-old Elizabeth. "He's a mite pindling, like me and my folks, the

Simondses," mumured the frail and gentle mother, apologetically. And although Nathanael might not have said it in so many words, for fear of fretting his young wife, privately he may have reflected that it was a poor time for an American colonist's child to come bleating into the world.

But it was a momentous time, a time of decision so great that it was bound to make a vast difference, one way or the other, in the character of the future life of one's little son. Why, as far back as 1766, even tiny Leominster's magistrates had drawn up an *Address* ending with a superb declaration—"we must, we can, and we will be free." Free? Nathanael Chapman was a militia man. Sometimes his trigger finger got a spell of the fidgets, what with all this talk and these dreams of freedom; and Nathanael but one of many who believed it could be won, at long last, only by means of trigger fingers, ready and loyal. An ominous time, and painful, for the stream of inheritance flowing between old England and young America was deep and strong. Yet the break was coming—war! How soon would the summons come, and Nathanael be off to battle, leaving Elizabeth the wife, Elizabeth the little lass, and son John?

Rugged days, and no silver porringer for a new baby, nor pewter either. Nathanael harvested the grains on his small farmstead, and he turned his hand to whatever carpentry job was offered, although little building was being done these days, so jumpy did everyone feel. Nathanael and his fellow citizens waited, trigger fingers itching, ears cocked for alarm. Indeed, a foreboding time to bring into being a Bay State child!

But by the morning light, down from the autumn-colored hills, the brooks flowed into Leominster village. "It's the very hour!" they chattered joyfully. "If young John Chapman is to become the one and only Johnny Appleseed when America goes free, then, by all the water sprites, this is the moment for him to begin his life! *Johnny Appleseed*—a name as folksy as a country fair, a name as catchy as a country tune!"

So sang the brooks of Leominster, in September's morning light.

1774-1775

II. MUSTER DAY

THE TOWN was astir early. For it was General Muster Day, when the militia would parade in martial review.

The crowd of onlookers was unusually large. They had gathered on the village green not only to enjoy themselves in holiday fashion, but for the comfort of rubbing shoulders with one another, of talking things over. Mouths were a little tight, eyes a little hard. Standing conveniently near the applejack booth, Jotham Johnson was holding forth in a loud voice, for as driver he was accustomed to shout above the clatter of the weekly stage to Boston and back.

"This new provincial government, now," thundered Jotham, "it's tough, praise be! Storing ammunition in secret places, so I hear. Mustering and organizing throughout the colonies, calling the militia *minute men*. That's good, by heaven! They'll go, on the minute, when the alarm sounds. Yankee doodle!" And Jotham laughed, grimly.

Azure blue arched over the town, unclouded. The village elms were like great parasols of pale yellow. In the hills, amid the everlasting green of pine and laurel, the oaks burned red with autumn's fire. The brooks gossiped softly. Old Nashua's shine was dazzling. Ah-h-h, how sweet the sound of fife and clarinet! The drums rolled. The cymbals clanged, shaking the air. Roll call pricked the crisp morning, sharp and quick as saber points. Inspection—the trainees clad ridiculously unlike: here the fine flared coat, there the buckskins, or the workman's smock. Some carried muskets. Some had only stout sticks. Yet they performed with a flourish. They were the minute men of Leominster, wheeling and marching in the name of the Commonwealth of Massachusetts. "Yankee doodle, by gum!"

Amid the crowd that edged the Common stood Elizabeth Chapman, watching her brother, Zebedee Simonds, and her husband Nathanael, both of the militia. Hugging her skirts was little Elizabeth, a sweetheart with big eyes. Presently the child would exchange her penny for a gingercake from the vendor. Yonder was the pie man at his booth. Pumpkin and mince and apple they would be to-day, and cider to wash them down. Piggins and baskets held rounded heaps of apples, ruddy and tempting. In this golden-ripe season, did not the apple reign as king of fruits—the *Roxbury Russet*, the *Winter Pippin*, the *Red Astrachan*?

Elizabeth Chapman carried her new baby John. Under his swaddlings his fists curled tight and pink as apple buds. Although he was not yet a month old, Elizabeth's thin arms ached with his weight. *La, la,* she was always strangely weary. Could she hold out the length of Muster Day? As if in answer to the thought, her two young sisters, Rebekah and Ruth, threaded their way through the crowd. Ruth took the baby. Now Elizabeth could give her full attention to the people around her. Her look was eager. She was only twenty-six.

Oh, it did her heart good to see such a sociable crowd on the Green this fine morning! Besides the country folk who had been streaming into town since cock-crow, and the

humbler villagers, there were the grand ones who wore
the ruffled shirts and the silver buckles. But what about
the Chapmans? Indeed, little John might not be gentry,
but he came of good Bay State stock, bless him! Elizabeth's people, the Simondses, had been on this side the
water since the first of them came to Woburn, around
1635. There they had stayed until Elizabeth's own parents
moved to Leominster and reared their nine children.

Nate's ancestor, Edward Chapman, Yorkshireman, had
settled in Ipswich in 1639. Elizabeth laughed softly to herself. Her sisters glanced at her questioningly. *"Ipswich,"*
murmured Elizabeth, "it's a name that always makes me
want to sneeze."

"You're wool-gathering, Bet," chided Rebekah.

Well, anyway, that long-agone Edward Chapman had
been a well-fixed man. For the cost of a sea journey to
America was nothing to make light of. Besides, a man must
bring along enough clothing and supplies of all kinds to
last him a year. So Edward Chapman did it, and he got
himself a nice farm at Ipswich (*kerchoo!*). When he died
he left, among other bequests, "thirty good-bearing apple
trees" to his wife. After Edward, Nathanael said, there
had been a John Chapman straight down the line until
he himself came along in 1746, at Tewksbury. When
poor little Nate was only six years old, his mother died,
she who had been Martha Perley. *Oh, how sad,* thought
Elizabeth, suddenly taking her baby, *for a mother to leave*

her children forever! And a breath colder than October's
seemed to brush Elizabeth, like that from a great, dark,
sweeping wing. She shivered.

However, Nate had never talked much about his youth.
He always said the best moment of his life was that August
day in 1769, five years ago, when he had married his love.
Elizabeth smiled. The sun was warm again. "Look at that
sea-blue sky. Listen to that brave music. Our small Elizabeth! Our little son!"

So Muster Day of 1774 slipped away into the sunset.
Autumn shook down all its golden leaves. Winter—and
the brooks of Leominster lay ice-bound, their chatter silenced. But within Nathanael Chapman's little house that
stood scarce a stone's throw from the Nashua, there was
an absurd cooing and gurgling as baby John began taking
notice of things around him. Small maid Elizabeth was
escorted to Dame school, trotting along the Broad Road
and across the Great Bridge, for with tall letters did Leominster honor its thoroughfares. Spring of 1775 came
early. The town was suddenly afroth with blossom. Again
the brooks gossiped their merry way to the river.

April the nineteenth. A balmy day, and a Leominster
lad named Joshua White, so the story goes, invited two
young sisters to go boating. How pleasant to float down
the river with a pretty miss, the sun glinting on the wave-
lets, the willows dipping their new green veils into the

shallows along the shore—but with *two* pretty misses! Spring does lay a lavish spell upon a lad!

They came to where the river broadened into the mill pond, a pleasant place, the birds flying over, and the plash of water falling like music from the great turning wheel of the mill. Suddenly from Leominster came the sound of guns. The oars froze in Joshua's grip as the voice of the American Revolution spoke its summons to him. "The alarm!" whispered the Misses Wheelock, their cheeks turning white as snowdrops. The alarm all New England had been waiting for!

And while the three listened tensely, the boat drifted on, unheeded. On to the brink of the dam! Joshua, suddenly sensing danger, had barely time to turn the boat end-foremost before it plunged over the cataract.

Someone in Leominster, then, or later, composed a ballad about that boat ride. The final verse goes like this:

> But White being strong, and meeting no harm,
> He took a Miss Wheelock under each arm,
> And carried them both safely ashore,
> Then bid them good-bye and said nothing more;
> But hastening home he snatched his gun,
> And traveled off for Lexington.

Razzing Joshua White, the minute men of Leominster carried rough merriment with them as they trudged off to battle. The incident lightened their hearts, sore with parting, grim with purpose. Among the ninety-nine who marched were Zebedee Simonds and Nathanael Chapman. Elizabeth was left in the house by the river, to care as best she could for her son John, now seven months old, and young Elizabeth.

1775-1776

III. THE DARK WING

AFTER A few days of service Nathanael Chapman, with most of the men who had answered the first alarm, returned home. The Lexington skirmish was over; the British back in Boston; the spring plowing was waiting.

But presently it was seen that this thing of winning liberty must be pursued and finished, for good and all. Nathanael enlisted for eight months in the Continental Regiment of Foot. By June 17th these troops were helping to fight the enemy from Bunker Hill. After the battle, Nathanael returned to Leominster, and on the 25th, a Sabbath, he and Elizabeth were taken into full communion in the Congregational Meeting. The children were baptized. One never knew—life was uncertain. It was well for the young Chapmans to be right with their God.

The winter of 1775–76 was as harsh as a New England winter can be. The wives of Leominster's soldiers suffered untold hardships. Neighbors and kin lent Elizabeth what aid they could, but often she must plow through knee-high snowdrifts to reach the outbuildings. The ice-coated Nashua filled her keeping-room with its chill breath. War had sent prices soaring. Elizabeth must watch every penny, every bit of bartering. She was a Simonds, naturally delicate. Daily she grew more frail. A racking cough made her nights wakeful.

Another April—1776. Another June. And on the third of that month Elizabeth sat down to write a letter to her dear husband, who was now at General Washington's headquarters in New York. For days Elizabeth had mulled over in her mind how she could express herself. She must be calm—perhaps Nate would always keep this letter. She would not spot it with her tears. Oh, she had wrestled with the Lord, even as Jacob wrestled with the angel: "Lord, Lord, however can I leave my babies?" Nate would get along somehow. She had reconciled herself to that. But her children! None but their own mother could love and care for them so mother-like. Yet, how useless, wrestling with the Lord! She had given up at last. Now her hard-bought peace strengthened her as the quill hovered over the sheet of foolscap. She began writing slowly, carefully, and as so often during these past months, she felt the sweep of that dark wing above her bent head.

Nathanael Chapman did keep Elizabeth's letter. It reads:

Loving Husband—

These lines come with my affectionate regards ... hoping they will find you in helth ... I am no better than when you left me but rather worse, and I should be very glad if you could come and see me for I want to see you. Our children are both well through the Divine goodness. ... I rejoice to hear that you are well and I pray you may thus continue and in God's due time be returned in safety. ... I send this letter by Mr. Mullins and I should be glad if you would send me a letter back by him. ... If you cannot [come to see me] I desire you should make yourself as easy as possible for I am under the care of a kind Providence ... I desire humbly to submit to His Holy Will ... patiently to bear what he shall see fitt to lay upon me. My cough is something abated, but I think I grow weaker, I desire your prayers for me ... that I may so improve my remainder of life that I may answer the great end for which I was made, that I might glorify God here and finally come to the enjoyment of Him in a world of glory. ... Remember, I beseech you, that you are a mortall and that you must submit to death sooner or later and consider that we are always in danger of our spiritual enemy. Be, therefore, on your guard continually ... and so I must bid you farewell and if it should be so ordered that I should not see you again, I hope we shall both be as happy as to spend an eternity of happiness together. . . . So I conclude by subscribing myself, your

Ever loving and affectionate wife,

Elizabeth Chapman.

Elizabeth folded and addressed the letter. *To Mr. Nathanael Chapman in New York in Capt. Pollard's Company of Carpenters. The favor by Mr. Mullins.* On the outer folds Elizabeth added news of a more earthly nature:

Brother Zebedee is well and is in Boston. Father's family is all as well as common. Mr. Johnson's famely is well. The widow Smith's and Joshua Pierce's folks are all well, and all our friends are as well as usual.

I have not bought a cow for they are very scarce and dear and I think I can do without, and I would not have you uneasy about it or about any money for I have as much as I need for the present.

On June 26th, the youngsters John and Elizabeth were wide-eyed with wonder when one of their aunts, or perhaps the widow Smith, showed them the new brother born that day. He was named Nathanael. Such a fretful wisp of a baby! As the days went by, Elizabeth was too weak for anything save the hard effort to breathe. What if the American Congress had boldly adopted a Declaration

of Independence? The colonies in their gathering greatness: Leominster in its dear familiarity: her own household: even the precious children—all seemed to be reced-
ing from Elizabeth, as if she saw them, small and dim, from
the far height of a soaring wing. On July 18th, three days
after the town Clerk had recorded the country's momentous decision, Elizabeth Chapman died of consumption.
Infant Nathanael soon followed her.

And so was left motherless the toddler, John Chapman.
Among his Simonds kin a lonely child, one might guess,
often dreaming of his mother in that "world of glory."
And it was in Leominster, with its river and its brooks,
that Johnny first learned to love and to follow flowing
water.

1777-1790

IV. IN LONGMEADOW

IN 1777, Nathanael Chapman reënlisted for three years.
He was made captain of a company of wheelwrights,
which in the course of time was stationed at the arsenal
at Springfield.

Extending south, following the superb sweep of the

Connecticut River, and along its eastern shore, lay a long strip of rich bottom land, called by the early plantation "ye long meadowe." (With what grace, and yet with what simplicity, did America's settlers bestow place names!) And where the river broadened to its greatest width stood the village of Longmeadow. Here lived a girl named Lucy Cooley. Whether she was rose-lipped and dewy-eyed, or the plainest kind of miss, no one knows. But she caught the fancy of Captain Nathanael Chapman, and married him in July of 1780. She was eighteen, the captain thirty-four. The next month he was honorably discharged from the army. He and his bride settled in with Lucy's mother, a widow but four years older than her new son-in-law. Although there is no actual record of the captain's motherless children coming from Leominster, to call the tiny house "home," it is highly probable. Johnny Chapman's first steps westward!

Nor could there have been a region more fascinating for any boy. First, there was the great river, which offered Johnny the delights of swimming and skating, and lured his mind, as rivers were ever to do, with their reach to the far and the unknown. On the Connecticut moved the flatboats, carrying fish and furs, hemp and lumber. Where, oh where, were they going, their clumsiness redeemed by the glory of their great white sails? A boy with the fever of vagabondage in his veins—why, even if he could have but a ride across river by ferry, what a wonderful sensation of space it gave him! Johnny's young nose that was someday to be as knowing as that of a fox, sniffed the wildness that was woods and water.

At Longmeadow there was the annual excitement of the shad fishing in spring, the nets spread on the Common to be mended; next, the hauling in of the catch; the parceling out to every fisherman, and finally the salting down of the rich harvest for next winter's eating. There were apple trees, from which the boys gathered fruit for the cider making. On the high land to the east, the woods invited adventure. A boy's days were filled to the brim in Longmeadow, and on the holy Sabbath he sat in the meeting house, gazing up at the Reverend Stephen Williams, an aged minister both beloved and famous. How difficult to imagine him as he had been at the age of ten, when he was taken Indian captive from the Deerfield settlement upriver! Oh, that was a tale so dreadful as to cause Johnny's scalp to crawl, and his hair to rise up like broom bristles! But the beautiful thing about the old minister, Sabbath-enshrined in the hand-carved pulpit, was that he bore no grudge against the Indians for their terrible violence against him and his family in that long-ago day. Only mercy and aid he gave them. Perhaps Johnny saw, with a child's clear perception, the beauty of charity shining like light in the aged minister's face. And perhaps a ray of that glory fell into his young heart, one day to enrich a strange dedication of Johnny's own.

So must Longmeadow have laid fingers, light or heavy, on Johnny Chapman. He learned his *a-b-abs* in the little red schoolhouse, and learned them well, although it frets an outdoor-loving boy to toil over his letters. But—"shame on you, now, if you can never make out to read the Holy Scriptures!" For Bible reading in those godly days was the end and aim of all learning. Therefore, Johnny must study his Dilworth Speller and his New England Primer, that by-and-by, when he went over the mountains, he might carry a Bible, and understand it, and live by it. Slowly, too, the boy learned to write his name, *John Chapman*, that he might someday make more than his mark on deeds to far orchard lands. Only, of course, while he was a very little tyke, he hadn't the faintest notion of such things.

And it is quite possible, yet perhaps naught but a writer's fancy, that one day the schoolmaster, tiring of the everlasting round of readin', writin', and 'rithmetic, brought an apple to school. It made an eye-catching brightness as it lay on his high, pulpit-like desk. At last he silenced the noisy blab-study of the children. He impaled the apple on a sharpened stick, and lit the stub of a candle. Holding them high he intoned, "Scholars, behold this apple! It is like unto the planet Earth, on which we dwell. See how it spins on its axis. Thus does Earth spin in infinite space. Note how the apple revolves around the candle's light, which represents the great sun. My poor mortal fingers soon tire of spinning the apple, but God's unwearied Hand guides earth's turning, in time that hath no end." Then the master, in a voice of thunder-and-lightning, commanded the children to think upon God's vast power and glory, and at the same time to remember that they themselves were miserable sinners. For in those days a schoolmaster was likely to clap a dreadful warning or a spine-chilling moral on everything he said.

But Johnny Chapman scarcely heard the warning. He was too full of young wonder, looking up at the turning apple. What a lovely roundness it had, shining now with day in the light of the sun-candle, now with night! And as may happen to a dreamful child, it made a lasting picture in Johnny's mind—the apple turning in space like Earth, and the master's guiding hand the Hand of God. Only he was a bit mixed up, being perhaps not seven years old. *Earth is an apple*, thought little Johnny. *Earth is a round apple.*

Johnny was eight when the Revolution was over. The next year England ceded to the new United States of America all the territory south of the Great Lakes and east of the Mississippi River. That vast frontier—what vast ideas, what great visions it inspired in American minds! Did young Johnny Chapman also dream of it as a far-off, hoped-for destination, as many boys must have dreamed? In 1787, when he was thirteen, the Ordinance was passed for the government of the territory northwest of the Ohio River, a region that Johnny was to know like the palm of his hand. The Constitution of the United States was drawn up, and two years later was declared in force. George Washington was made first president. Great and growing times for a growing boy!

By 1790, when Johnny was sixteen, there was a crop of up-and-coming half brothers and sisters in the little house at Longmeadow, so many that Grandma Cooley would need to count and name them by thumping them, rather mockingly, perhaps, with her thimble. It was a good thing she decided to move away from that swarming household, for there would be five more babies within the next thirteen years. And *la me suz*, in a few years, if Grandma Cooley didn't catch a captain of her own, and marry him! But Johnny's sister Elizabeth was an old maid of twenty-nine when she married Nathanael Rudd, of Charlemont, a town on the Deerfield River.

As for Johnny himself, growing more long-legged every day, it was time he was earning his own bread. And the truth of how he first went about it is a key that fell out of the pocket of Johnny's youth, and was forever lost. Some say that while he was but a little shaver he sold herbs and peddled his father's handmade woodenwares through the countryside—pails and bowls, spoons and skimmers. Some figure that he may have been apprenticed to an orchardist, learning early to sow and to plant, to reset and distribute. Else how, they ask, could Johnny have become enamored of apples, and of a mission as curious as ever came to rule a man's life?

He was from the first an odd, independent sort, his folks always said. He didn't often tell where he had been the livelong afternoon, or if he was seen coming out of the woods or up from the river, what he had been doing. However innocent a boy like that may be, he and his secret ways can puzzle and vex a family beyond all bearing. It's likely that Lucy Chapman, bone-tired and overburdened, shouted above the clamor of her babies, "Johnny Chapman, if ever there was a queer 'un, you're *him!* Why can't you be like other folks?"

But "like other folks" Johnny would never be.

1792-1797

V. JOHN CHAPMAN
SETS FORTH

LET'S GO West, Nathanael. Let's you and I go."
John Chapman's eyes glittered with the "western fever." He was eighteen, his half-brother Nathanael but eleven, and this was 1792. The story goes that the two boys set out for Olean, a small settlement in west-

ern New York State, where an uncle lived. Here they expected to break their journey, but found Uncle's cabin deserted and himself gone a-pioneering. They moved in and spent the cold months.

This story is said to have been founded on family traditions. It has appeared in print more than once, and print has a magic persuasion all its own. But there are no facts to verify it. And half-brother Nathanael, as one sharing Johnny's travels, fades away like a small ghost. We do not actually see him again until he is a young man in Ohio.

It would not be the least surprising if the brothers had caught the fever to do some gadding of their own. So many folks were on the move, now that the Revolution was over, leaving everyone a good deal poorer in pocket, but incredibly richer in country. For years the boys had heard the big talk of travelers who stopped at Longmeadow's taverns, *The Red Horse*, and *Ely's*, on their way to or from Boston and New York. The brothers heard also the *Gee's* and *Haw's* of the ox-team drivers on the Connecticut Path that jumped the river at Springfield.

"We'll be going on 'til we come to the Hudson River," boasted the drivers. "We'll cross at the Kaatskill. And God willing, we shall come at last to the Susquehanna, and there we'll bide, less'n we take the notion to fare onward. Great country, this! Just to think on its stretches the mind fit to burst. And it's our'n, 'cept for lickin' the Indians and the Alleghenies. But plenty of folks've already

got over those mountains, and their young 'uns singing at
the summit:

> Oh, I've often heard them say
> That there's lions in the way,
> And they lurk in the Allegheny Mountains, O!

Lions—that's just a jokey word for brushing away the
fear o' bobcats an' panthers, lad.

"Or, we might go on to the Northwest Territory. Its
got two counties a'ready, Washington and Hamilton, and
a score of settlements with blockhouses. But those plaguey
Indians—they're fixin' to make some real mischief, hear
tell, and we're right fond of our own scalps. So fare ye
well, lads, we're off to the Susquehanna, and mebbe some
day, when it's a heap safer, we'll be heading for the Ohio."

"Nathanael," whispered Johnny, "it does seem if you
follow the rivers, they will take you 'most anywhere."

By the early or middle 1790's, young John Chapman
was working as an orchardist as far west as the Susquehanna region of Pennsylvania. "West" it was, for the center of population was then a few miles east of Baltimore.
To the coastal dwellers of Johnny's youth the West was
the Hudson gorge and Oswego and the River of Apples in
the wild Chautauqua lands of York State. The West was
the Wyoming and Lebanon valleys and a web of streams
that led to the great westward-flowing highway of the

Ohio. The West was Tennessee and the brand-new state of Kentucky. It was a wall of mountains and the promised land on the other side. It was prairie, fertile and ready. It was forest, and the itch for a leveling ax in the hand. It was the lonely cabin, the sparse settlement in the clearing, the blockhouse and the faraway fort. It was massacre and unspeakable savage cruelty, and the slow but sure rout of the Indians from their hunting grounds. The West was a driving hunger that set wheels and hooves and feet in motion. It was a promise to sons and daughters—"You will have fields and orchards of your own. You will found and build cities." The West was aching farewell and perilous adventure, hardship and hope and faith. It was a great dream. And the heart of it was a freedom such as men had never known before.

If you follow the rivers—did an American lad of the 1790's realize that history was then taking such long, earth-shaking strides? And that he, however humble, ran by its side, believing, sharing, creating? The strides led ever westward, by river and trail. By trail and by river young Chapman would go to the far new Ohio country. Hadn't George Washington been fighting and working for it through the years as a place for American settlement? Yes, Johnny must go as soon as the Indian wars were over. He must go, now that he had walked westward out of his boyhood in the old Bay State—now that his legs were long enough to walk with the largeness of history, with the smallness of a man's own intensely important choice of adventure or of mission.

John Chapman had a mission. It was an odd one, but as important to him as a man's can be. It had nothing to do with disappointment in love, or with being kicked silly in the head by a horse. For by such dramatic explanations did myth-makers try, in later years, to account for Johnny's queerness. They did not guess how his mission burned in his young mind, pure as flame, strong as courage. And the chalice that held it was Johnny's religion.

Johnny's boyhood had been shaped by piety. The little meeting house; the divine light in an old man's face; in a boy's heart the wisdom of the Bible, which he had learned to read when very young; his mother's farewell words— *that I might glorify God*—long had he treasured them. And probably in these early 1790's, but before ever he had begun to plant orchards on the frontier, Johnny had taken up a new faith, so new that its followers in America were then scarcely more than a handful. They called themselves Swedenborgians.

Their faith was based upon the doctrines of Emanuel Swedenborg, Swedish baron, scientist and inventor, who, while searching for an explanation of the universe, had come upon God. "Heaven was opened to me," declared Swedenborg. With that, he believed himself divinely appointed to "unfold the spiritual sense of the Holy Scriptures," and he devoted himself to the writing of many books on the subject. His followers founded the Church of the New Jerusalem.

Young John could not have been lacking in intelligence to have interested himself in the intellectual doctrines of this new creed. Perhaps he did not understand the whole of it, but in his own way he made use of the heart of it. And the heart of it was love—the love of God for man, and of man for God—love of all creation in a universe wherein the spiritual world is as real as that lesser one in which we move. John Chapman, burning with a mystic's zeal, became a dedicated man. With the only skill he possessed, that of an orchardist, he would faithfully serve the pioneers. With them he would go into the wilderness, yes, even before them he would go, to plant the trees which would someday drop their fruit into welcoming hands. Love of all creation—it was as simple as that for simple-hearted Johnny.

So in November of 1797, John Chapman, now about twenty-three, left the Susequehanna region. Following West Branch and Sinnamahoning Creek he entered the present Pennsylvania counties of Potter and Mc-Kean. His goal was the twisting Allegheny River, the wild Allegheny country. Now he may have gone up into York State to Olean, for it was a little place of boat building and the head of navigation for the river. It is said that he also visited the shores of Lake Erie at this period.

However that may be, it took Johnny a full month to travel from Wilkes-Barre to the Allegheny, afoot and alone as he was. So, years later, said a certain Judge Wetmore of McKean County. But whether the Judge heard Johnny tell his own story, or heard it from others in the way of legend we cannot know. Johnny was no hand to talk of himself, ever. He saved all his shy eloquence for apples and heavenly grace. But supposing Johnny was drawn out for once—in truth, when a man who has made a sacred vow sets forth to fulfill it, traveling alone through majestic wilderness, may not his pilgrimage become exalted and heroic in his mind, like that in a saga?

1797-1799

VI. ON THE FRONTIER

"JUDGE, it was time I was heading West," Johnny related. "History had already oldened itself, with Harmar and St. Clair defeated and the Indians running red-handed through the settlements, a-firing and a-scalping, while the white folks who'd been hankering for the West cooled their heels at the borders, or were bottled up in the blockhouses, waiting. Then General

Wayne built his string of forts from the Ohio to the
Maumee. He fought and won. He had a treaty made at
Greenville. The land was opened and safe for the new settlers. They came by the score and there's still no end to
them, what with the wilderness so vast. Back in '97, even
as now, Judge, the needs of the pioneers had a grip on my
soul, and I a lad in buckskins with my blanket and my
tommyhawk, heading West. That was before the love of
all creation had taken such hold of me that it banished my
fear of man and beast. So I carried a rifle, as men do who
venture forth with more trust in their trigger-sight than in
God Almighty. In my knapsack I had my Bible and the
fixin's I thought I'd need, and at night I slept with it under
my head, for there were seeds in it, Judge, precious apple
seeds. I'd sorted and washed and dried them out of the
pomace pouring from the cider mills of the Wyoming and
the Shenandoah. They were my treasure and my hope.

"So I followed the Pennsylvania waterways, and I took
the portage trails, now frozen, now deep in mud, while
November rattled the bare branches of the woods. Sometimes I fell in with emigrants. Sometimes I slept at cabins
that stood fewer as the harsh miles dropped away under
my feet. 'Where you boun' for?' asked the men, every
time. And when I'd say no place in p'ticular, but in the
service of God to all places in the West good for planting
and for pioneers, they'd not say much, but look at me sly
and sideways, like as if they thought I was touched in the

head, or else a poor shifty body. 'Where's your wife and children?' asked the women, every time. 'In heaven,' I'd answer, 'waiting as my reward when I'm through with traipsing this green earth by my lone.' For a woman seeks to nest down her young 'uns, and a little space of her own to tidy up, and didn't I know that John Chapman would all his life be as homeless as the wind?

"But the children never asked me any such sharp questions. All they wanted to know was how soon my seeds would turn into apples, and their eyes bright as chimney sparks in the asking. Trust and faith—that's what children are, Judge, and they make a man feel mighty humble.

"Sometimes I'd leave one of my little deerskin bags at a cabin, if it appeared the folks would value the seeds, though there were already some orchards bearing in that country, seeing as parts of it had been settled long enough, and an apple tree always first to fit in as natural and homey as home-folks in their own home place.

"Early in December I reached Warren. 'Twas nothing then but a clearing among the great oaks, with a blockhouse, and settlers nigh as scarce as hen's teeth. I stayed there, looking around to find me a place to plant, come spring. I was all of a pucker to sow my first seedlings on the frontier. But a planter learns to get a lasting grip on patience, trusting the seasons, and Nature. *By the breath of God frost is given ... He scattereth his bright cloud.*

"There was little open bottom land in this country then,

Judge, for the forest lifted right up from the streams, dense as night-shadow, and every tree a pillar of mighty growth. And animals—why, man alive, the land was theirs, pretty nearly. I've heard tell of cur'us beasts in foreign parts, marked and shaped fit to witch a nightmare. But those times in the wild Allegheny woods, before the settlers took the gun to 'em wholesale, I saw the noble elk, the buffalo and the panther, the black bear and the timber wolf—an endless differing of beasts down to the little raccoon and the weasel.

"I found open ground on Big Brokenstraw Creek in this county of Warren, and while the streams were still full of broken ice I sowed my seeds. Judge, that was the first planting I did on the frontier. Praise be, the seedlings I nursed there stand today full-grown and fruiting on many an Allegheny home place."

The Judge said that the settlers of Warren County were too few at that time to make any sizable demand for Johnny's trees. And while he was ever ready to give them to those unable to buy, he expected to sell now and then. Johnny was no beggar, and was he not obliged to eat? So he moved sixty miles down the Allegheny to Franklin, once Venango, an Indian town, and afterwards the site of a fort which had in time flown the flags of three nations. Now it was a meager settlement, nestling among towering wooded hills, its small activities centering in George Powers' trading post. The Indians were friendly, for by this time the wars were over, and Captain Fowler held the old fort without troops. Big, honest John Martin, who ran the ferry, and Colonel McDowell up French Creek, were true types of the hardy pioneer.

The region seemed promising, and in the rich margins along the creek and river the young apple planter, pointed stick in hand, thrust his seeds. But a history of Venango County, published in 1890, scornfully dismisses Johnny's sojourn there:

John Chapman, who took up land in different parts of the township [French Creek] *but whose sojourn, owing to his thriftless disposition, was only temporary. He appears to have been impatient of the restraints of civilization, so much so, that as soon as the settlements began to increase he disposed of his few improvements, and with a few other spirits as restless ... as himself, drifted further westward.*

Benighted historian! It was never Johnny's intention to settle permanently in any one place. In Venango County Johnny had accomplished what he had come to do. He would move on. Must not the cheeks of his bough-hung apples shine in the reflected light of a hundred flowing streams; waterways as lovely as their names—the Monongahela, the Muskingum and the Kokosing, the Maumee, the Wabash and the Kankakee?

Traveling south and southwestward, Johnny became a

familiar figure in Butler County. At last he must have
come to where the crumbling ruins of old Fort Pitt over-
looked the Ohio, that great river of his westward-bearing
dreams. For John Springer, who later moved to Ohio, said
that he first became acquainted with Johnny when the latter collected pomace at an old cider mill near Springer's
house in Pittsburgh. Back of the fort the wedge-shaped
borough sprawled toward the hills. Johnny would have
felt "woods-queer" in bustling little Pittsburgh. It has
been said that he was employed there by General James
O'Hara, whose house stood amidst the orchards that were
once a part of the King's Artillery Gardens at the fort.
Did Johnny work for hire among the hundred apple trees
of the King's Gardens? A story frail as petals falling.

Johnny frequented western Pennsylvania for many
years. Even after Ohio became a habit with him he kept
coming back. For Nature takes her own unhurried time
with seeds and growth. Johnny was duty-bound to re-
visit and tend his nurseries.

Often he allowed his trees to grow up in their birthplace for the use of whatsoever creature passed by—man
or deer, squirrel or bee. Generally he took up his two-year
old saplings, packing them in wet moss or earth, and leaving them at some trustworthy "station" agreed upon, tavern, trading post or cabin. Many were outright gifts. Some
were exchanged for food or clothing. A little money now
and then, a promissory note, perhaps undated, because

Johnny said he might not be around to collect at the time specified. Or, the payee might not have the money handy just then, see? Johnny had a lovable sort of indifference to such details. He was what is called "unworldly." It is a quality often mistaken for a lack of common sense.

Down into Westmoreland County Johnny traveled, and to Greensburg. His heart beat high as he trudged up the rough slope of Main Street, not because of the happy shouts of the boys playing on the Common, nor because the creak of the smithy's bellows seemed a social sound to a lonely pilgrim. No, it was Mr. John Young, Esquire, whom Johnny was so eager to see. For, in a way, the gentleman was Johnny's own kind, being a Swedenborgian.

Mr. Young now welcomed Johnny as if that young man were a personage. Accustomed to judging men accurately, Esquire Young saw before him a missionary so zealous as to be willing to face great hardships, and he saw a friend worth having. In the firelight that flickered on the Judge's parlor hearth the two men must have talked together, softly but glowingly, as do those who share with ardor the same beliefs. Long and late they talked, the Judge in his lawyer-like method making clear whatever doctrine Johnny did not understand. They talked, in the Swedenborg way, of the unseen world which lies almost within sight and hearing, and how, in one whole and perfect moment, a man might catch a fleeting glimpse of it.

They talked of the mission field. John listened spellbound when the Judge told him of James Glen, a Swedenborgian missionary of brilliant mind, but of extreme poverty, for he had given all he had to the poor. "James Glen lives in a hut in the Demerara region of South America," said the Judge, "where he is called 'the Swedenborg hermit.' The Indians come to him from far and near for healing, for baptizing, and to hear him preach. A true hermit of the wilderness!"

"A John the Baptist!" breathed John, overcome with this word-picture of so holy a Swedenborgian. In his secret heart he was to idealize it all his life, hoping that a bond of likeness linked John Chapman, in the Northwest Territory, and James Glen, in the woods of Demerara. Yet John would never be completely the hermit. Sooner or later his Yankee push and his devotion to apples and to pioneers would draw him out among men.

"I will act as your agent, John, in sending you the New-church tracts, both for your own reading and for distribution among the settlers," promised the Judge, at parting. "Here is a packet of them. Now farewell, my friend, and God go with you."

So John took up his way again, and if he had been a shade less zealous, he would have gone shouting *hosannas*, so filled with the glory of renewed inspiration was he, so longing to give. Like James Glen he would carry healing herbs to the frontier—snakeroot, dog fennel, mint and garlic. Flower seeds, and the miracle of their blossom by the cabin doorstep: the Swedenborgian tracts, the Bible, and the beauty of their sacred words. And apples—why, glory be!—his mind gathered their names into a bouquet—*Sweet Bough: June-eating:* the golden *Russets: Red Gillyflower: Seek-no-further.*

At Flushing, Long Island, William Prince's nursery had been flourishing and famous among the colonies and in England for some fifty years. In Virginia, one Thomas Grimes gathered the first pale sunny globes that would bear the name of *Grimes' Golden,* an apple enduringly loved. Out in the Territory, at Cincinnati, at Marietta and Belpre, there were new apple orchards, and there were new towns springing up—Dayton, Zanesville, Cleveland, Chillicothe. New government tracts were opened for settlement—Donation, the Military lands, the Fire lands. A fellow named Daniel Converse was carrying the United States mail along Zane's Trace from Wheeling to Limestone in Kentucky.... Yet—wolf and Indian, swamp and forest and prairie—how wild, how far! ... John Adams was president. George Washington died and was buried at Mount Vernon. *Brother, O brother, whatever shall we do without Father Washington?* And the people, already half-forgetting, scrambled over the mountains and poured down the rivers into the promised land.

The largeness of history, the smallness of a man's own choice of adventure! Now was the time. Now, from the cider mills John Chapman must gather many, many apple seeds to carry into the Territory. There was a new press, he'd heard tell, about seven miles below West New Town, on the Youghiogheny. It was owned by one Metzger, a farmer orchardist. John came to the river, and followed it downstream.

1800-1801

VII. WITH MAGIC ON HIS BACK

THE POST roads from Philadelphia, Baltimore and northern Virginia came together at the little log settlement of Wheeling. They scrabbled down the cliffs in muddy troughs to the boat yards and wharves on the big river. From the cliffs Appleseed John saw the broadhorns and batteaux, the keel and flatboats floating their freight of emigrants, animals and goods. Other travelers came into town by road and trail, either to embark here and continue by water, or be ferried across to pick up Zane's Trace on the Ohio side. Zane's was known to the Indians as the Old Mingo Trail, and was someday to become a part of the National Pike. In 1800, it took the traveler stumbling and fumbling uncertainly through quagmire and forest until, if he were fortunate enough to reach Chillicothe, he might branch off on other trails to gain at last the goal his vision held.

From Wheeling, Appleseed John also beheld in mid-river Zane's Island, with a road across it, and ferries on either side. There was Colonel Zane's island house, his farm lands and his orchard saplings, some of which were to bear a famous apple called *Zane's Greening*. Here, within John's immediate vision were the things that mattered most to him—orchards and pioneers, and that which only the young planter could see—his resolve to serve. And now, during the first year of a new century, when he was twenty-six years of age, John Chapman plunged into the Ohio wilderness.

Some say that he went by way of Zane's Trace with a horse-load of apple seeds, planting as he traveled. For instance, it is told that before ever the first settlers arrived in Guernsey County (then a part of Muskingum) someone had already been there. Some unknown solitary had built a tiny cabin and planted a small orchard on a ridge lying between Buffalo and Duck Creeks. Who planted and built? The Guernsey grayheads always stubbornly insisted that it was Appleseed John who in the long ago planted the little orchard between the whispering streams. But perhaps that was because, like all "westerners," they wished to claim for their own region the legend of Johnny

Appleseed's sowing.

Some think that the young planter came into the central Ohio wilderness by river, first to Marietta, where the lovely sycamore-hung Muskingum flowed down to meet the broad Ohio. Marietta—a fortified town founded by Revolutionary soldiers representing the best of New England. In their hearts lingered memories of Rutland and Middletown, Danvers and Ipswich. In their new habitations were the old home treasures—the great family Bibles, the snuff and spice boxes, the pewter ware, the iron kettles. But now, with gun and ax and hoe, with courage and determination, but against great odds, hands and minds were occupied with the building of a city and the vast domain of the Ohio Company. Now, in 1800, the cluster of cabins at the Point was growing. Corn and vegetables grew lush among the huge tree stumps. The first rigged vessel, built at the new shipyards up the Muskingum, was even now sailing with a cargo of pork and flour down the Mississippi for the open seas and a Cuban harbor. Marietta was port for the passenger packet which made regular round trips between Pittsburgh and Cincinnati, although it was no more than a keelboat fancied up. The tin horn of an occasional floating store sometimes brought the Marietta women flying down to the waterside. The settlement was a post exchange, the mail coming and going in a long narrow vessel built like a whaleboat, steered by a rudder, the crew armed to the teeth. Men were prospering from trade in furs and ginseng, beeswax and maple sugar.

Appleseed John saw it all with the eager curiosity of the young traveler who carried in his mind the dream of a fabulous West. Campus Martius he saw, high above the Muskingum, with its blockhouses and dwellings behind sharpened palisades. He marveled at the ancient fortifications and mounds which the local Indians declared had been built in the world's morning-time by a race of giants.

But organized settlements such as Marietta had little need of Appleseed John. That he knew. In this big Washington County, landholders were pledged to plant at least fifty apple trees within three years of settlement. The promise of fruit, therefore, was already green along the slopes of the Muskingum and Duck Creek. On the fertile meadows at Belpre, Aaron Putnam had a fine young orchard, sprung from scions packed in beeswax and brought over the mountains on horseback. *Pound Royal: Golden Pippin: Roxbury Russet: Putnam Sweet*—did not their very names speak both bravely and poetically of the transplanting of New England husbandry to the new land?

John dropped downriver to have a critical look at the Belpre orchards. "You say you don't believe in grafting trees?" asked Aaron Putnam, in amazement. "That only God can improve fruit? Now I remember—you're the fellow I heard of over in Marietta—*Appleseed John*, folks call you. Well, Appleseed John, you go your own way with apples. I'll go mine. It's a free country, praise to our fighting fathers!"

So Appleseed John would carry his sack of seeds into country where only the native wild crab bore its heavenly bloom and its puckery fruit. And the young traveler carried another bag. It could not be seen, but the farther he went, the more plump it grew, for it was a bag of stories. John gathered them at mill and cabin, at tavern and trading post, not with intent, but as a traveler does when meeting many adventurous persons in exciting country, and during a thrilling period.

"Man alive," boasted the Mariettans, "such fish as swim bug-eyed in these western waters! Why, one summer, 'bout ten year ago, Gilbert Devol gigged a pike that weighed ninety-six pounds! Our tongues don't burn us in the telling, either, for it's God's truth. When Gilbert came up into the settlement to show off, he had the fish hung from his shoulder, holding it by a stick run through its gills, and the critter so danged long its tail dragged the ground. Folks were tongue-tied with wonder, 'cept someone—we forget who 'twas—asked in a slow, comical drawl—'Is King Pike taking a Devol for a walk? Or is it t'other way around?' Well, we had the big fellow roasted—we mean the fish, not Gilbert—for the Fourth o' July barbecue that year. And 'twas pretty near enough for everybody. Since then, many's the pike been taken from the water close to the size o' that one.

"In the winter of 1793 three of our men killed forty-five deer in one day among the hills. Yes, this is rare hunting country. No wonder the savages come back every fall for it. During the Indian trouble they went hog-wild with spite, killing the animals wholesale to try and starve us out. Pretty near did it, too."

From Marietta and the Ohio, John slipped away as quietly as he had come. For while he was in this country he had a mind to go up Duck Creek way and see his kinfolk, Levi and Sally Chapman, who used to live in Saybrook, Connecticut. In fact, John found such a gathering of Chapmans at the Forks, and such welcome, that he took pen in hand and wrote to his father, back in Longmeadow. "Yes, urge Nathanael to move out here," advised Cousin Levi. "Tell 'im we've cleared things out a bit since we came a-pioneering in 1794. Tell 'im the bottoms along the crick are rich as velvet. Tell 'im we've petitioned and got us a road to Marietta. Tell 'im we've got mills. Tell 'im the Indians are pushed up to the northwest, 'cept when they come hunting. Tell 'im," added Levi, as one Chapman to another, "that I'm constable of this township."

"Tell him," piped up Levi's grandson, little Thomas, "that we named a crick when we first come a-pioneering. Guess what we named it?"

Levi laughed and ruffled Thomas's hair, fondly. "This little shaver wasn't born when we came. Not by two years. But when he heard the story he took such a notion to it that it's fixed in his mind he was with us, bless his boots. You see, Cousin, it was on a New Year's day when we stopped alongside a stream to eat. So wasn't it as natural as drawin' breath that we'd name the run New Year's Creek?"

Thomas's lip trembled. Grandfather Levi had taken the boy's favorite story right out of his mouth. Appleseed John drew the pouting little fellow to his knee. "That water had been flowing there since time was," he said, gently, "and never with a name to it. Wonderful it was, now, for a pioneer like you to give it a name when you chancied along."

"New Year's Crick," repeated Thomas, happy once more. "It's a keepen'd name. For always, it's keepen'd."

"John, tell Nathanael, your father," began Levi again, "that there's no end to the hunting hereabouts. Plenty of bear and deer and smaller game, though not much elk and buffalo any more. Killed off, or mebbe wandered to other parts.

"Reminds me, Cousin John, soon after we pioneered, a young fellow named Moon was hunting in the Hockhocking river country below us and west. Springtime it was when Moon killed a mother buffalo. Brought her calf to his place and gave it to his milch cow to raise. Had 'er plumb puzzled, I guess, for pretty soon that young buffalo fetched up a pair o' shoulders bigger'n any calf she'd ever laid eyes on. Moon was mighty much tickled with his pet, and he got to thinking how clever it would be of him to take the buffalo over the mountains to show to folks in his old home town and on the streets of cities.

"So, one morning 'fore sunup, Moon set off with a halter around the buffalo's neck. That was the last we heard of 'im 'til about two weeks ago when word sifted back as to what befell.

"Seems like all went jim-dandy at first, the buffalo as meek as a lamb, and the people everywhere gathering to stare, and to hear Moon hold forth on the marvels of the backwoods. At first he was dressed in buckskins like we 'uns, but presently he was diking 'imself out in fawn-colored pantaloons and satin weskit and a neck cloth bigger than most, for the coppers were raining *clinkety-clink* into his hat.

"But the time came when the buffalo's real nature began b'ilin' up inside of 'im. Then didn't the coppers fall thick as hailstones, what with the crowds pushing and shoving to see a beast so dangersome? First he was fretty. Then he was fractious. Moon set out to use a goad on 'im, and with that 'twas said the buffalo's eyes burned with hate as red as live coals. When he lowered his horns an' pawed the earth an' snorted 'twas enough to lay a crust of ice along a body's backbone.

"Well, 'tain't a pretty story. For one day the beast charged Moon, head down, tail up, nostrils breathing fire, so the Danvers folk declared. Anyway, then and there the buffalo made an end of Moon. The Danvers militia hustled out and fired a volley. And that was the last of the buffalo."

"All from the sin of killing the mother buffalo in the first place," commented Appleseed John, sadly; though he was quick to drop the buffalo story into his bag. "Every one of God's creatures has a right to live."

"Pshaw, young man!" exclaimed Levi. " 'Tis a question that's never been threshed out. In the meantime, what can we do but take the animals for food and fur? And may our bullets fly with more cunning than that of the wolves and foxes that prey on our stock. I see you're an upright man, Cousin, but for a proper Chapman you've got some queer notions and ways. I fear you'll get yourself talked about in this new country. And it's unlikely you'll ever make a success of yourself," Levi added, anxiously, "with never more than a bag of apple seeds to your name."

"*I have a goodly heritage,* Cousin Levi," answered John, quoting from his favorite book. "*The Lord is the portion of mine inheritance.*"

There was no arguing with the Scriptures, not even when one heard it from a queerish kinsman. The cousins parted with good will. Levi promised to send John's letter to Longmeadow at the first opportunity, and John left some of his religious tracts for the Chapmans and their neighbors. With the two magic bags on his back, the one of seeds, the other bulging with the babble of story tellers, he struck across country to the Muskingum again, following

its narrow winding valley northwestward. Above Water-
ford and Wolf Creek mill, the country grew more primi-
tive and rugged with John's every step. For all his faith
and courage, did not his spirit quail at the thought of the
vast unknown ahead of him?

Oh, the wilderness bared its dark savagery to the traveler—the overpowering somberness and silence and loneliness! It sprang its cruel surprises—the loss of the trail and
the delirious wandering: the entrapping vine, the ensnar-
ing thorn; in the air the tormenting mosquitoes; underfoot
the sudden rattler; at heel the ravening pack. But there
was also the breath-taking revelation of its primeval majesty, the lavishness of its centuries-old growth. Young
Chapman's dream of the fruitful orchard danced ahead of
him in the moted shadows and above the floating stream.
Also, his mood was ever curious. Now, with the river
leading him he dilly-dallied and he zigzagged. Here he
chanced to meet a chain of surveyors, there a trapper.
This night he slept in some Indian village, wrapped in his
blanket. And meeting so few to talk to, perhaps he began
calling out greetings to the animals that crossed his path.
"Ahanh, fellow, you'll get a ketch in your back, skittering
away from me like that! And you and I brothers! See? I
have no gun. . . . So we meet of a sudden, old man, and
which of us the most pimple-skinned with scare! I call
you Bruin, but by what name do you call me? Nothing
good, I reckon, for off you go! . . . There, now, you pretty

bird, shaking the bright drops from your wings, have done, and whistle a tune to lighten my loneliness."

And if John Chapman turned a little crazy in the years to come, might not a man, who walked so rough a path of self-sacrifice, and whose forest-shadowed thoughts dwelt on the things of God too vast and dazzling for his comprehension? There was also John's constant pains to guard his body against destruction. The fellow threading the pioneer wilderness with a gun on his shoulder was doubtless a brave and daring one. But the fellow *without* a gun—was he not courageous beyond imagining? The wolves, those cowardly but most persistent and savage of all American beasts, had no knowledge of the sweetness of Johnny's spirit. It was Johnny's body they slobbered for.

But now he came safely to three tiny settlements, one of which was called Zanesville. Here the Licking River met the Muskingum. John would follow it. What kind of country did it water?

It was country such as we Americans dream of when we think in heart-hushed wonder of the early days. Forest tall and dense as night, with grapevines as thick as a man's body twisting among the trees and hanging out their clusters of purple fruit in warm Septembers. A myriad of spring-fed streams, crystal clear. Ancient mounds of the Indian dead, and pole cabins of living Wyandot and Delaware and Shawnee at Raccoon and John's Town, at Brushy Fork and at Bowling Green. A prowl and skitter of animals, and so many snakes they crawled into the cabins and the beds of the first pioneers. In 1802, a huge den on the riverbank was blown up with a charge of gunpowder.

When Appleseed John came, there were only three families in what is now Licking County. One of these belonged to Isaac Stadden, a German from Pennsylvania, whose wife, two children and brother, Colonel John, shared his cabin. Brother wanted a wife. Where was he to find her, for mercy's sake, unless among the wood nymphs? But she came before the year was out. Betsey Green and the Colonel had a Christmas wedding, Judge Smith coming all the way from Zanesville to perform the ceremony. Did Appleseed John join the handful of wedding guests and prance across a puncheon floor to the fiddler's tune of *Peel the Willow?*

Young Mistress Stadden, wife of Isaac, had a mind of her own. Fancy her, now, roundly scolding Appleseed John.

"I speak wot I tink, Chon Chapmans. And I tink a strong yong man like you it vos too bad you do nuttings but traipse from here to avay and from avay to here. What dis contry needs already are sober peebles to settle down mit a vill to clear de land and build de towns. Apple-trees? Now, look, Chon Chapmans, at dose liddle tree saplings I carried in my chist all de vays from 'S'vany. Dat's de vay apple trees should grow oop in a new land—homebodies dere own selves, mit your own kinder to play around dem, and your own frau to gedder de fruit and boil it down in a kettle a'ready. Ya, I don't like it so vell you vaste your life planting trees out in de noveres, to be vashed avay mit floods or eaten oop by rabbits. And how vos you to keep yourself decent-bodied in de voods yet? Shust look at you dis minute. Na, I don't like it so vell."

John held no grudge. It was not his way. Catherine Stadden was a fine woman. Justly proud she was of her whistle-clean cabin, of its furnishings ably made by Isaac, who was by trade a carpenter. A responsible, forward-looking woman who strove to make Newark, which grew up around her like a colony around the queen bee, a progressive, God-fearing city. But perhaps, with a secret little chuckle of amusement, Appleseed John tucked into his story-bag one he may have entitled *Bigfoot Joe's Courting*. For every season the Indian *Bigfoot* came to the Stadden cabin, bearing gifts of furs, maize, maple sugar and nuts, berries and ginseng. Would Isaac trade these valuable things for his strong, fair-skinned squaw? Patient was Bigfoot, asking. Patient was Isaac, refusing.

Presently Appleseed John wandered off by his lone among the vast thickets and deep ravines of what was later Maryann Township, planting an orchard in the wildest country he had yet penetrated. But he failed to fence in his orchard. In a few years the cattle of the first pioneers had destroyed it. Did Catherine Stadden's scorn of John have anything to do with the failure of his first planting in Licking County? And was it because she looked askance at his travel-stained, long-haired shabbiness; was it because her trestle top was scoured so bone-white and speckless that John formed the habit of declining to sit at table with the pioneers, eating instead from a bowl as he sat on the hearthstone, or outside on the doorstep? Or was it only because, as the days of his singular life went by, humility grew on him like bark on a tree?

Within a few years Isaac Stadden had a fine young orchard of his own, on land farther down the valley. For a long time after John had become Johnny Appleseed, he kept returning to the Stadden farm. Catherine's heart was warmer than her practical German mind. She made him welcome, always. He and Isaac were ever good friends. They had apples to talk about—the *June Red*, *Zane's Greening*, the *Punkin' Sweet*, the *Fall Wine*.

Part II
THE FRUIT

The following stories are based upon both truth and tradition. Some of the young characters were once real persons who knew, or who might have known, Johnny Appleseed. Each story bears the name of an apple of Johnny's day.

1799-1800

FALL WINE

OLD TRIGGER the dog roamed restlessly among the men gathered around the cider press. Suddenly he froze to attention, then bounded off toward the woods that edged the Metzger farm to the north. For a moment he stood taut, nose up, one foot raised, asking quick silent questions of his experienced old hunting self. But not even when he began barking did anyone notice him much, except Nancy Metzger and her friend Billy, from up Jacob's Creek.

"Now what's that old fussbudget hollering so loud about?" asked Nancy.

"Dogs know more'n you think," answered Billy. "Maybe Trigger's after something important," he added, as the last half-inch of the dog's tail disappeared into the tangled thicket which flanked the woods. "I could go and see what 'tis." Billy dug his bare toes into the soft earth to keep himself from the folly of going.

"You'd better not," warned Nancy, seeing through him, but allowing him to strut. "It might be a bear that would drag you off no-telling-where. It might be an In-

53

dian, who would slice your scalp right off your head."
She shuddered, seeing in her mind's eye Billy's shining
brown crop pathetically dangling from a savage belt.

Billy lifted his hand and touched his hair. It was fastened
on tight, safe. "Look!" he cried, happily. The underbrush
at the forest edge parted. Out came Trigger, at peace and
wagging his tail. The children, gazing beyond him at the
hidy-hole from which he had emerged, saw the leaves
quiver again, a stirring scarcely more than a bird would
have made slipping from twig to twig.

"We'll keep an eye peeled," said Billy. But in a little
while they had almost forgotten. To watch the cider
gushing from the press was of such unfailing interest. The
fruity smell of it made the boy and girl wish they could
ladle it, dripping from the gourd, to their lips once more.
But they were already filled to the brim with apple juice.
Billy even had the beginnings of a misery. He wouldn't
pay any heed to it unless it made him double up and
bleat. He did see, kind o' slantways, Trigger darting into
that secret place again, but no snoopy old dog was going to
drag Billy's attention away from the last exciting stages of
the cider making.

Yesterday the men had brought their own boatload of
apples to Metzger's mill, coming from up around West
New Town. Before dusk had fallen the fruit had been
ground. Billy and Nancy could see the circle of tracks
made by Pepper, the work-horse. To grind a quantity of

apples took two or three hours of Pepper's patient circling of the mill, standing within its big framework of timbers. The heavy horizontal lever went round and round with Pepper, and the wooden cylinders drew in and crushed the apples. The pomace had lain in the vat all night, a thick fruity sandwich between wooden blocks cushioned with straw. This morning the juice had been pressed out by means of screw and hand-lever. Frederick Metzger, orchardist, had made the mill and the press himself, all by hand, all of wood. Now the men helped him to pour the cider from the pans into the plugged barrels they had brought, which they were soon rolling downhill to the river bank. *Slosh, gurgle* sounded the cider from within the turning barrels. Heaving them into the boat, the men called back, "Send word, Fred, when the Bishop gets here. We'll come to preachin'." They floated downstream.

No sooner were they out of sight than there came an exclamation from Granny Metzger. She had brought a chair from the house and was enjoying the fine autumn day while stripping beans from their pods. "Law!" gasped Granny. " 'Tain't the Bishop, now! 'Tain't anybody I know. Steppin' out o' the woods thataway ain't uncommon, but all the same there's something uncommon about it, or about *him!*"

The children's gaze followed Granny's. "Pa!" called Nancy. She stepped quickly to the house door. "Ma! Comes a stranger."

All eyes turned toward the woods. With Trigger trotting alongside, as if the two of them were lifelong friends, a bearded young man was advancing from the leafy covert. There was something shy and humble about him, yet innocent and free. Neither Granny, nor Pa, nor Ma could have explained it, but he reminded them of a forest creature that is both timid and trusting. His eyes brightened as they rested on the children. "This is the place I've been aiming for," he said. "Metzger's?" His voice was quiet, but warm with proffered friendship.

"I'm Fred Metzger. Welcome," greeted Pa. He held out his hand, a little sticky with apple juice.

"Peace and safety to all," said the stranger. "My name's John Chapman."

"Welcome." Pa said it again. "I'm just about to clear out these leavings." He loosened the screw of the cider press, and as the cylinders separated, took up his wooden shovel to draw out the shrunken form of the pomace.

"I'll help," offered John Chapman.

"After dinner," objected Ma. "Come in, now, and sit by." Her glance included the new arrival.

At the table the Metzgers bowed their heads. "Will you give thanks, John?" asked Pa. It was courtesy, gentle and pure.

"Lord, Thy bounty to Thy children is everlasting. We give Thee thanks for the sustenance of earth's fruits and heaven's promise. Let the glory of Thy love shine on this house, and on all Thy creatures."

"It's nice to have a stranger settin' with us," thought Ma, her heart strengthened by the prayer. From the steaming kettle on the hearth she dished up.

"Stewed squirrel," whispered Billy, his eyes bulging with joy. But his spoon and that of everyone at the table paused in mid-air when the Chapman fellow refused a helping from the kettle. "I eat no meat," he excused himself, gently. "It means the taking of life."

"Now, now!" protested Pa, himself taking a hearty mouthful. "Then what will you have from our table, man?"

"This corn pone is beyond compare," answered John. "A body could want nothing better than these boiled turnips. Milk sustains." He stole a look at the pies on the table. "My mouth waters, ma'am. Apple?"

"From the first of the *Fall Wines*," answered Ma.

"The *Fall Wine* is a prime apple," declared John, his eyes sparkling. "The apple—any apple—is the king of fruits."

"Fred's pa and me—we brought that *Fall Wine* apple up from Virginny when we moved to this Westmoreland frontier fifteen year ago," remarked Granny. "And other kinds. When we set forth we buried the young trees in a cart half-filled with earth. Every time we forded a little stream, we'd pull our tree-wagon into deeper water to soak the roots. Them little Virginny saplings was the beginning of our big orchard out back. It's Fred's now that his pa's gone. Young man," demanded Granny of their guest, "where do you keep?" She couldn't hold her curiosity a second longer.

"I don't keep, permanent," answered John. "I roam."

"From where at?" persisted Granny.

"From West New Town. I worked in the boat yard there the month past. Before that, from Greensburg. I have a friend there." John's face glowed as he spoke of Judge Young.

"And before that?" nagged Granny.

John shifted uneasily. He was shy of so much attention. "From Pittsburgh, ma'am," he answered, patiently. "And from the Erie and the Venango country. From the Wyoming valley along the Susquehanna." He might as well get it all out.

"You've come far, for a young fella," observed Pa.

"You must've been born somewhere," hinted Gran. *Plague take* such a close-mouthed man, forcing a news-starved granny to ask endless questions.

"In Bay State. Leominster. But I was raised and went to school in Longmeadow. Earth is an apple. Earth is a round apple."

Everyone looked startled. A little touched in the head—this stranger?

The stranger also was a bit surprised, although he kept it to himself. What a far thing to remember! What a little thing to remember, after all these years! He couldn't have told why it had burst from his lips. The mention of school at Longmeadow, perhaps, and the memory of the schoolmaster turning an apple in his hand. The heady fragrance of apples at this orchard on the Youghiogheny. A man's love for apples. John quickly changed the subject. "Twins?" he asked, nodding toward Nancy and Billy.

A laugh went around the table, like brook water over stones. "Billy belongs to the folks at the Alliance Iron Furnace, up Jacob's Creek," explained Ma. "He's a-visiting."

"I wish I was home," groaned Billy, suddenly. "I've got a misery." He pushed back his chair, creeping crank-sided to the outer door. He collapsed on the step, doubled over and bleating.

"Too much cider, I misdoubt," mourned Ma. "And squirrel and pie top o' that. Now the colic's got the best of 'im."

"Give me leave to cure the lad." Young Chapman hoisted Billy and carried him to the yard. Kicking over an empty barrel he laid the moaning boy over it, face down. And while Trigger went dog-crazy with excitement, John rocked the barrel back and forth, keeping a firm pressure on the small of Billy's back. The motion and the pressure had the same effect on the boy as a violent sea voyage has on a poor sailor.

"I've heard of that trick," said Granny, cackling with

glee. "But I never saw it tried." Pa was laughing fit to bust. Ma laughed, too. "The stranger's a handy man to have around," she remarked. But Nancy only stared. It seemed a queer thing to make a boy well by making him sick.

Billy was soon right side up again and on his feet, a little wobbly, but smarting out to scuttle his recent unmanliness. "I feel so good I could kill a bear," he boasted.

"We thought you were a bear in the woods, Mister," said Nancy. "Or maybe an Indian."

"Or even the Bishop," added Granny.

"We're looking for Bishop Newcomer any day," explained Pa. "When he comes he will give us a preach in the log meetinghouse I built yonder to draw such as him, or any circuit-riding preacher. We're holdin' our hunger mighty precious for the Bishop's preaching."

"You've built a shelter for preaching?" breathed John. His eyes burned like fire coals in darkness. "Preaching is like bread to the famished," he said. "God speed the Bishop to come while I am here."

Pa showed the meetinghouse to John, the children tagging along. "It's nigh as bare as the new-borned," said Pa. "But I made the pulpit and the slab benches myself." He showed off his orchard, too, the trees now thick-hung with apples. "I've got to start picking right away," Pa said. "I ship to West New Town. From there the fruit goes by flatboat to the market at New Orleans. I save the poorest apples for our own cider making."

John nodded. He seemed to know all about it. After the press was cleared out, he said, "By your leave I'll be taking the pomace to the river to wash and sift out the seeds. I've got me a tow sack for straining."

"Take all the seeds you've a mind to," granted Pa.

"Young man," called Granny from her chair. "You talk like a downright orchard grower. Be you?"

"I have no full-grown orchards yet," answered John, "but many small nurseries from Erie down to Wheeling."

"Do tell!" cried Granny. "I would never've 'lowed you to be one whose fingers stick to the shillings."

"I plant for the needy and the have-nots," explained John. "For the pioneers in the new wild land."

"My sakes alive, and what do you get out of it?"

"Joy and salvation," answered John, humbly. He was off to the river with his pails of pomace, the children following.

"Now what do you make of 'im?" Granny demanded of Ma. "An odd piece, if you ask me."

"Bless him," whispered Ma. " 'Joy and salvation'!" She lifted radiant eyes to the blue sky. "My!" she exclaimed, softly, "seems to me I never saw such a pretty fall day."

Watching John down at the river, Nancy observed thoughtfully that seeds do not appear to be important.

"Seeds are precious," answered John, reverently. "Apple seeds in p'ticular, but all seeds. I mind when I was up on French Creek there was a woman named McDowell. A pioneer she was, and couldn't abide anything getting the best of her. She kept chickens, and great store she set by them for the sake of the eggs and sometimes an old biddy stewing in the kettle. Summers, she raised a garden patch, although it was hard to come by the seeds and she was mighty saving of them. One day when her folks had relished a ripe melon, Mistress McDowell washed the seeds and set them out on the doorstone to dry in a pan. Along came one of her little old biddy hens. The mistress turned around in the nick of time to see it peck up the last seed.

"She flew into action. She wasn't going to lose those precious seeds. No, siree! She chased that hen and she chased that hen. And after considerable hysterics on its part, it was caught. Then didn't the mistress take up a knife and slit the biddy's throat, neat and quick as ever was? And didn't she squeeze those melon seeds out of Biddy's crop, every last seed?

"But of course she wasn't going to lose her dear chickabiddy, either. So she sewed up its throat with her needle and thread, as a lady sews a fine seam, only mighty quick. She set the hen down whole and alive. Off it skedaddled to join its mates, and fell to scratching and pecking as if nothing had ever happened!" John's eyes twinkled as the children raised echoes with their laughter.

They were at his heels every minute, Billy refusing to go home as long as "the appleseed man" stayed on. He told them stories out of his boyhood; of the boat ride on Leominster's millpond the day Johnny's father marched off to Lexington; of the Indian captivity of Stephen Williams. And he told them of a narrow escape of his own.

"It was the time of the Indian wars, when red man and white had only hatred for one another. I had gone up into the Erie country to see some famous apple trees. For when it comes to apples I'm forever curious. These were Indian trees, of great age and size. Where they stood had been a come-togethering place for time out o' mind. Of feasts and war dances and councils, those trees could've yarned a-plenty.

"After I'd talked with the old trees and got the seeds from a core or two, just for pleasuring myself, I did a little meandering, for I'm curious about country, too. It was wild as lonesome, there. One day a couple of Indians spotted me. They set out for me lickety-split. There was no time, nor use, either, for me to signal that I held no grudge against them. My legs could do my only argufying just then, if I was to save my scalp. So my legs ran, and they ran swift, dodging from tree to tree. After a while I came to a swamp, and by that time I was a good piece ahead of the Indians. There'd been a hard storm the day before. A big tree had blown down and part of its trunk and its wide-spreading leafy branches lay out over the edge of the swamp. I waded into the water and went under, flattening myself backward against a submerged limb. The leaves hid me, and I breathed through the hollow stem of a plucked reed. They grew thick in that swamp. The tip of the reed, above water, brought air into my lungs. It was an old trick I borrowed from the Indians themselves, and from white hunters.

"Presently I felt the fallen trunk tremble under the tread of the Indians. Looking up through the water and from behind the leaves, I could see those dark, fierce faces peering down. For when I waded into the water, the mud of the swamp had risen in a brown stain which told on me as sure as footprints tell. The Indians seemed to peer beneath every twig. The longer they searched, the angrier they grew. I scarcely breathed, but in my heart, where speech is voiceless, I prayed. And God saved me. Finally the Indians gave up their search. I stayed in that watery hidy-hole until deep in the night, for fear of their tricks. How I ached when I came out! But I got out of that region in a hurry, and when I reached Oil Creek, I laved my soreness with the healing oil which floats upon the water."

"That Johnny-man only talks real free when he's off with the childer," grumbled Granny, "an' me with a craving to hear all his words. They've got a shine to 'em, somehow."

"When he gives thanks at our board, or reads to us at candle-lighting, his words are fit spoken as 'apples of gold in pictures of silver,' like the Bible says." Ma flushed at hearing such beauteous words falling unwontedly from her own lips. But the next time it came handy, she asked the stranger, "Happen you ever do any preaching?"

"I once missionated in the Potomac country," answered John.

"Tarnation!" cried Granny. "Keeping a thing like that to yourself, and me from an old home-place in Virginny!"

"Never mind, Gran!" chided Ma, quietly. "I'm thinking John might give us a preach come Sabbath, seeing as how we've no news of the Bishop."

"I couldn't exhort elegant like a bishop," said John. "But if I'm asked to take the stump and preach the Word, it's my bounden duty to do it. God will give me grace."

"Praise be!" said Pa. "I'll send the call to the neighbors."

In the meantime the apples were gathered, Pa and Ma and John stripping the trees, Granny and the children picking up the fallen ones. Cresting baskets of the fruit were stored in the meetinghouse. The cider press yielded up its foaming juices. The barrels were plugged, ready for shipment.

The Sabbath came. In Metzger's meetinghouse John preached to a handful of backwoods folk. His words lacked the thunder of the Bishop. Yet he held his listeners spellbound, gently, strangely. Their tears fell as he described the glories of Paradise awaiting the righteous. And it seemed comforting and entirely natural when he spoke of apples with the same bright zeal. For did not their harvested fragrance fill the meetinghouse with testimony of God's gifts to mankind—to themselves—man, woman, and child along the Youghiogheny?

Soon after that John Chapman said he must be traipsin' along, for he hankered to plant some nurseries in the Northwest Territory. The children felt desolate at the thought of saying farewell. And while they watched for the last time his work with the seeds, a far, faint call came from deep in the forest. "Halloo!" answered the children, their voices so wafer-thin the air swallowed them at once. "Halloo-oo!" shouted John, cupping his hands. He told the children to wait at the house. He would go into the woods. Perhaps someone was in trouble. It was two hours before he returned, and he was not alone. "I've brought you a bishop," he announced, twinkling a little.

"I was mired in the cedar swamp," explained Bishop Newcomer. "This young man—this Appleseed John— found me."

" 'Appleseed John'!" cried the children with delight. "Why, we ourselves've been calling him 'the appleseed man'!"

"*Appleseed John*—he's known as such by everyone along the frontier, as I've discovered in my travels," said the Bishop. "Coming through the woods we've been arguing, but without anger, he for the Swedenborgians, I for the Lutherans."

"And for God," added John. "The trees listened."

Such odd things as Appleseed John said, thought

Nancy. *The trees listened.* Come to think of it, trees do have a listening way with them.

"We'll have preaching, Metzger," stated the Bishop, "as soon as word can be spread. And marrying and baptizing."

So the Bishop preached in the log meetinghouse. With thunder and fire he preached. The very rafters shook. The benches trembled under the quaking listeners. The apples shivered in their baskets. It was "a blessed, fearful, soul-stirring time," said everyone.

But after the Bishop had ridden away, after Billy had gone home, after Pa and Appleseed John had set forth with Pa's boatload of apples and of cider, Ma said, "The Bishop's preaching makes a body go hot and cold. It turns the soul inside out, and we're the cleaner for it. But the Chapman stranger's ways and words—they were queer—yet they had something in them you're likely to tell about a long, long time from now."

"You needn't tell me, Ma," declared Nancy. "I'll remember my own self."

For it was only the other day that Nancy had sat in the meetinghouse, on the slab bench with the other children, gazing up at the appleseed man. A strange mortal, who could say things which seemed strange and lovely to a child. And on preaching day his talk of fruits and of heaven seemed blended with the aroma of Pa's apples, as if they were of the same essence, sun-warmed and flavor-some, homely and simple. Always she would remember Appleseed John, when she saw and smelled the apples of autumn. *Fall Wine, Bellflower, Early Harvest, Front Door.*

1805

FRONT DOOR

THE STUMPS left by the road builders were as big as table tops. Young Andrew McIlvain trod alone and manfully among them. Although but thirteen, he was an old hand at it. For once every week, by round trip, he followed the rough new road between Franklinton and Chillicothe. The weight of the bag on his shoulders was a proud burden, for it was nothing less than United States mail, and he its first carrier on this route. The United States, youthful, but strongly growing, and a boy of the wilderness in its service!

However, Andrew would have scorned to apply the word "wilderness" to this part of the nation. Was not Ohio a state these two years, and Chillicothe the capital, with a little stone-built state house, and a spreading number of dwellings? Every month it seemed that the little mail bag grew heavier, what with important papers being rushed to and from Governor Tiffin. Andrew might some day have a longer route, but he would never have a more important one.

From Adam Hosac, Contractor and Postmaster, Andrew's father had secured this appointment for his son. Afterward, Pa had pointed out Andrew's faults, not to Mr. Hosac, but to Andrew himself. "There's two of you, boy," said Pa, gravely. "One's a lad that's duteous and work-brickle a-plenty. The other's a notionatin' boy with fancies too queer-shaped for everyday. Why, I was not much older'n you when I enlisted as a Continentaler. Eager for it, too, but so young and skinny I had to stuff cotton in my hose to fill out my shanks. *Cotton Legs*, my mates called me. Son, this country's moving too fast to have any truck with a notionatin' lad-o'-dreams. So I 'low this job will do you good. See that you're good for the job. Here's your gun. Here's the mail to guard with your very life. Now, light out, and God bless you!"

Andrew, returning today to Chillicothe, shifted his gun. He was not afraid to use it in defense of the mail, and of himself. There'd been an evening when he was well-nigh scared out of his wits by wolves, and almost within yelling distance of the mill where he was to stay the night. He'd followed his route with scarcely an hour's loss of time when he was shaking with the ague. In freshet season he'd been obliged to swim the swollen waters of Darby and Deer Creeks, holding gun and mailbag high, by sheer strength. Seemed as if the cricks were bound to get the best of Andrew McIlvain and the United States mail that time. All the same, Pa didn't know, maybe, that Andrew was still sometimes the "notionatin' " one. The route was frequently deserted for miles. The blast from the boatman's tin horn echoed up from the Scioto far too seldom, so that the lonely trace often became a pathway for a boy's long dreaming. The loneliness was the hardest to bear, and sometimes the forest seemed to become too big and too dark for Andrew. He'd seen strange things and heard strange sounds, or thought he had. He gave himself a sudden shake. He began to sing a song which had been written for the Scioto Land Company, a song designed to draw New Englanders away from their stony fields. It was full of bluster and raillery. It had in it a world of hope.

> When rambling o'er these mountains
> And rocks where ivies grow
> Thick as the hairs upon your head,
> 'Mongst which you cannot go;
> Great storms of snow, cold winds that blow
> We scarce can undergo;
> Says I, my boys, we'll leave this place
> For the pleasant Ohio.

Andrew ceased his singing, his lower lip dropping in surprise. For another voice was carrying the song onward, and the singer's mouth was still pursed roundly on the final whistle-shaped vowel of *Ohio* when he crashed out of the underbrush.

"Why, I remember you! You're Appleseed John!" cried Andrew, loosening his grip on his gun. " 'Bout three years ago you were in Chillicothe."

"Right," said the other, smiling. "But now I'm called Johnny Appleseed, I suppose because of planting seeds in more places and giving news fresh from heaven to more people—they feel better acquainted with me."

"News fresh from heaven?" queried Andrew.

"The word of God, lad, always welcome to the hearts of men," Johnny explained. "When I come the cabin people ask, 'what's the news?' For in the clearing news cheers like sunshine after rain. So after I've smoothed away the lonesomeness with all I've gathered and with tidings of other faraway lonely folk, I ask, 'will you have news right fresh from heaven?' And I get out my tracts and my Bible, and I read the holy Word. It's pure blessing, in the lonesome backwoods."

Here's one for barmie talk, thought Andrew. Yet the talk somehow pleased him.

"You carry news, too, boy," Johnny went on, "but set down by quill and printing press. Not so folksy as my tongue-talk of pioneers. Not so wonderful as news from heaven. But nation-important. You're young for carrying the mails."

"Makes me more work-brickle," explained Andrew, lifting his chin.

"I know," agreed Johnny. "Bet there's folks think it takes the notionatin' out o' you." He grinned as Andrew threw him a surprised look, crying, "D'you know my father?"

"What's the name?"

"McIlvain."

"Your pa's got a clearing up Paint Creek," Johnny said. "And now I remember you, too, Andrew. You've grown a sight in three years."

"Outside I'm like Pa. Spindle-shanked. If they'd be a war I'd have to stuff my legs with cotton 'fore I could be a soldier," declared Andrew.

"Looks like Tecumseh the Shawnee—" Johnny fell silent. His face was shadowed. "But lad, inside you're like—?" he queried, kindly.

"Notionated, like my mother, so Pa says." Andrew blushed to find himself talking so freely about his private self.

"S'pect you're lucky," murmured Johnny. "But you haven't said anything about this little fawn creature I'm carrying. Found it snagged fast by the creepers. Only half alive it is. I couldn't have brought it out if the bag of seeds on my back wasn't more than half full."

"What you going to do with the fawn?"

"I told it what to expect. I promised I'd give it to a little girl, kind, with eyes as gentle as its own."

Andrew's thoughts flew to someone he knew on Paint Creek. "My sister Megan would do," he ventured.

"Sounds befitten," cried Johnny, pleased. "That is, if your mother doesn't think otherways. I gave one to a child in the Mad River valley last year. She hung a bell from its neck. It followed her around like a pet dog."

"Ippy's my dog." How easy it was to talk to Johnny Appleseed! "He used to belong to Mr. Jervis Cutler, who runs the fur-trading station up the creek. Reckon Ippy is the oldest dog anywhere. S'pect you don't know that *Ippy's* short for *Ipswich*, Mr. Cutler's home town ayont the mountains."

"I wouldn't have guessed it, maybe," answered Johnny, "but I know of Manasseh Cutler and his son Jervis. They're famous in Ohio for having been among the first forty-eight to come on the *Adventure* galley to Marietta."

"Oh, but Ippy came on the second boatload!" Andrew boasted. "He was just a new puppy. Besides him, there were eight other dogs, two cows and their calves, seven hogs, and—oh, yes, some men. That's why Ippy is an historical dog. Mr. Cutler's told me lots of stories 'bout those times." Andrew suddenly switched topics. "Pa and us came up here from Kentuck in 1797. I was only five. Queer how I don't remember much, 'cept the sickness that laid low so many folks, an'—an'—I remember the Brannons like yesterday."

"You talk like a graybeard," twinkled Johnny. "Tell me of the Brannons." Anyone might have thought that Johnny crooked his arm just then to scratch his back, but he was loosening the drawstring of his coonskin story bag. A boy who was haunted by a memory would maybe tell a story without making it larger than life.

"This Brannon fellow came to the Chillicothe settlement," began Andrew. "And it turned out he had a light-fingered hand, for one night, when a man by the name of Crawford lay sleeping at the tavern, Brannon slunk in and stole Crawford's greatcoat, his only silk handkerchief and his fine cambric shirt. The next morning Brannon wasn't around. Neither was his wife. So the settlers put two and two together, and the constable and some others went to Brannon's old home in Kentuck. There he was, strutting about in Crawford's handsome clothes, and bragging how he'd made a heap of money in furs along the Scioto. But before he'd hardly got the last big word out, the constable had 'im trussed up on his pony, bound for Chillicothe. Brannon's wife, too, only not trussed.

"Chillicothe hadn't a state house then. We weren't a state yet. Court was held under the great big sycamore aslant of *Green Tree* tavern. A slew o' settlers from Chillicothe and up and down the cricks came to Brannon's trial. It didn't take long, because he'd already pled guilty. The judge gave 'im his pick of two punishments. One was a public lashing at the whipping post. The other was riding his pony under guard to every door of the settlement, where he was to say, 'This is Brannon, who stole the great-coat, handkerchief and shirt.' His wife was to lead the pony and listen to the sneaky words.

"So that's the punishment Brannon chose, though it was said afterward if he could have chose again he'd rather've suffered the whipping. I dunno, Johnny," Andrew went on, with a troubled, faraway look, "it made you sick to see that down-bent woman draggling through the mud, and her face greenish-yellow with shame. There was Brannon, trussed half 'is size and crooked-like on the pony, and the people at every door staring at him with faces as hard and still as stones. Not a sound could be heard in the settlement that day, 'cept the voice of the thief, saying over and over, 'This is Brannon, who stole—' "

"The sin of man, clothed and riding," sighed Johnny. "A dreadful foolish thing is sin, and sad, always sad." He looked at Andrew, and saw that strange and bitter pageantry of pioneer justice haunting the boy's eyes. "Now come, lad," cried Johnny, lightly, "shall we go singing into Chillicothe? I'll teach you a war ditty my father learned when he was a green young Continentaler."

> Come out, ye Continentalers!
> We're going for to go
> To fight the red coat enemy
> Who're plaguey "cute," you know!

.   .   .   .   .

Bill Sneezer, keep your canteen down,
We're going for to travel;
"Captain, I wants to halt a bit,
My shoes is full of gravel."

Ho, strike up music—for'ard march!
Now, point your toes, Bob Rogers,
See! Yonder are the red-coat men—
Let fly upon them, sogers.

"Johnny Appleseed!" cried Andrew, flushed with laughter as Johnny sang the final absurdity, "will you hand over the kitling fawn to Megan yourself, and bide with us a spell? There'll be an extra helping for the morrow's Sabbath dinner. Once she has the makin's, there's nothing scrimpity about my mother's cooking."

"And I be welcome, much obliged, son," answered Johnny. "I'll give your folks news of Ohio and of heaven. I'll make little sister acquainted with the fawn, and I'll meet Ippy the dog. Likely, if we hit it off friendly, he'll tell me his old-time history. Then I'll be on my way. I've got some little errands among the nurseries I've planted here and there these five years, and I'll wind up at Duck Creek Forks, for my people from the old Bay State are coming to settle there among our kin. There's a slew of 'em, with Sally the youngest but two years old. I've a hankering to see them all."

In Chillicothe Andrew left his mail bag at the post office. It was nothing more than a tall, railed-in desk at the tavern, with a stack of pigeonholes in a handmade wooden frame above. At once Johnny Appleseed was surrounded, both on his own account, and because of the young dapple-coated animal in his arms. While the innkeeper's wife was persuading the fawn to suck milk scooped from a pail with her fingers, the men asked eager questions of Johnny. With sparkling zest he talked of the settlements springing up in the region—Piqua; Springfield on Buck Creek, where Simon Kenton, the famous Indian scout and fighter, was now running a grist and saw mill; Franklinton, "a city in the borning," Johnny predicted. "And you ought to see Cincinnati on the big river," cried Johnny. "Mark my words, it will be the city of the West, give it a little time." Then Johnny hushed his voice and spoke of the new Indian village near the ruins of old Fort Greenville. "The Shawnees've built beyond their rights on the white man's side of the treaty line," he said. "That village torments the settlers roundabout like as if it was boiling hot mush in their mouths. Tecumseh and his brother the Prophet come there. They're a power among the Indians. They'll bear watching."

Johnny was asked about himself. "Been back to prune my orchards near Wheeling, and on George's Run and along the Big Stillwater this side the Ohio. Gathered seeds at Metzger's and at other large orchards t'other side. Planted a nursery for Thomas Grimes. And around these parts, to Stadden's, on the Licking. In 1801 I wintered up as far as Vernon Run with Andrew Craig, a wild fellow as ever was, in wild country. Keeps you laughing in spite of yourself, does Andy. He thinks one Indian's worth two white men." Johnny chuckled and went on. "Been over on the Little Miami and the Big. Planted along Wayne's War Road in Butler County. Even been a little ways into Indiana Territory. That's lone, unsettled country—the Whitewater—but pretty as a picture. I planted there," concluded Johnny, simply. "There will be apples waiting for those who come."

He and Andrew and the fawn went up Paint Creek to the McIlvain cabin, and found welcome at its door.

1805

NONESUCH

A SABBATH afternoon, warm and hazy. Leaves scarcely stirred. Creek water slipped noiselessly by. In a comfortable cool hollow between spreading tree-roots Andrew McIlvain lay half asleep, tired after carrying the mails. Pa, too, nodded on the door-stone. Mother was reading one of Johnny Appleseed's Swedenborgian tracts. Below Andrew on the creek bank, but half hidden by a lacy curtain of leaves, sat Johnny and little Megan. The fawn lay stretched the length of Megan's legs. Pointed ears and nose, snowy throat, its head was a charming profile within the circle of the girl's arms. The fawn's coat and Megan's hair were almost the same color. Their eyes were truly alike, big and dark and questioning. Megan's love for her new pet was a sight to behold. And Andrew could tell that she was uncommonly drawn to Johnny Appleseed. She sat in a trance of smiling silence, watching the fawn, listening to Johnny. The old dog Ippy listened too, his chin propped trustfully on Johnny's knee. And that hen of Mother's—the one that hovered the clutch of wild turkey eggs Pa had found in the woods—it was funny how close to Johnny the hen lingered as it scratched the earth. *Maybe the hen also listened,* drowsed Andrew. Amusing Sabbath-day fancies swam lazily through his mind. *Maybe—*

"Maybe you'd never guess, Megan," Johnny was saying, "how I'd like for you and my half-sister Persis to know one another. Then there's Barbary Bland, who lives not far from the Staddens. Born nature-sweet was Barbary, for her cradle was a sugar-trough and her home an Indian sugar camp 'til her father could raise his cabin. And you'd like Sally Ross, a merry tomboy on the Mingo Bottoms in Jefferson County. Sal was the first white child born in those parts. And where? Why, mind you, in a hollow sycamore. The Ross family of seven lived in that tree, so you know it must've been a big one. The rotted-out limb that reared up from it was the chimney flue."

"Don't you know any boys, Johnny Appleseed?" called out Andrew, sleepily.

Johnny reached into his story bag and did a little sorting. "Of course I do," he answered. "Now, here's Alexander, up along French Creek in Pennsylvany. Alexander's folks'd managed to raise a little patch of wheat on their clearing. Come harvest and they were plum' tired of cornbread and potatoes. Wheat bread—wouldn't that be tasty? It was Alexander who was sent to the mill to get the wheat ground.

" 'Twas near daydown when the lad started back home with the bag of flour across his saddle. At Hanna's Gap a big black bear broke from the thicket and planted himself on the trail, squareways and sot. The horse halted, trembling. Alexander shook like a leaf. He couldn't speak bear language, and all he had for a weapon was a measly little switch. His wits went into a spin. There was nothing to do but try to fool the bear by dropping the bag of flour. *Criminy*—it made Alexander's heart bleed to do it. Then he gave his horse a sharp cut with the switch and streaked it for home, leaving the bear sniffing at the bag.

"It was a terrible small and weepy Alexander who crept into his pa's cabin. Now there'd be no good wheat bread! Alexander's pa couldn't bear the thought. He grabbed his gun. He jumped on the horse. Back he tore to Hanna's

Gap. *Huzza*, the bear was gone! And the flour? Why, it was unharmed. Alexander told me himself that the wheat bread they had that autumn tasted a bit like a bear's snout, but all the same it was the finest he'd ever put in his mouth."

"Alexander should've had a good hunting dog," remarked Ippy, quietly, lifting his head from Johnny's knee. "Once I had a master with strong-striding legs and adventurous, square-trodding feet. A dog could trust those feet of Jervis Cutler's. He was the first among the Marietta settlers, by-the-way, to leap ashore. He cut down the first tree. He and I were young together. We shared a great relish for hunting." Ippy licked his jowls over *relish*.

"A good word, Ippy," encouraged Johnny. He glanced toward Andrew, calling out, "Didn't I say yesterday that Ippy might tell me a story? Oh, the lad's dropped off to sleep." Yet Johnny wasn't sure of it. There was the curtain of leaves, screening, yet delicate as a dream.

"If my young master sleeps, let him," advised Ippy. "I would not have him hear me speak homesick for Jervis Cutler. It's only that we old ones cherish the memories of our youth." Ippy whimpered softly. Johnny stroked him. "Go on, old fellow," he urged.

"Our first autumn," Ippy continued, "a chain of surveyors went out from Marietta to measure the land between the Big Hockhocking and Raccoon Creek. It was new country to all, very rough and full of exciting wild smells. For Jervis Cutler and I went along, he out of curiosity, and I for a dog's reasons. One day a couple of us dogs and our masters volunteered to go out after fresh meat for the party. Jervis and I went up one side of the creek. Benoni Hurlburt and his dog beat along the other side. Whatever game took to the water would be sure target for one of us. We came to the Little Raccoon. Jervis thought it was still the main stream and followed it. I must confess I had a dog's boding about it, but Master was master. We lost the trail. Jervis told me if he fired Benoni might hear, and answer. But no, he'd save his powder. We'd surely find our way back to camp. That night he shot a bear. It galloped away, wounded. 'Twant like other bears I'd met. It didn't tree itself. I lost it in the woods. Jervis and I felt pretty hang-dog about that bear!

"Dark time. No supper. Master built a fire at the foot of a dead beech. And *dog my hide*, Johnny, while we slept, if the flames didn't skite to the very top of that tree! I jumped up, barking, just as a piece of burning wood dropped to Master's chest. Poor man, how he tore at his hunting shirt! All the rest of that long night, he tossed with pain."

"Pity I wasn't there to boil him up a plaster of beech bark and leaves," Johnny deplored. "It's the Indian cure, mighty healing."

"Endless dog-trotting next day," Ippy went on. "No game, for the dry leaves rustling under our feet gave warning to the wild creatures.... Another day. Now we were in burnt-over Indian hunting-grounds. We saw where deer and buffalo had lately trampled the wild pea vines, but not one animal came within sight. I found and ate a shrew. But what good is a dog's nose unless it serves his master? Three days now since mine had eaten.

"That evening I found a starved young 'possum. Hungry as I was, I turned away from a helping when master had roasted it, for 'twas no more than two poor mouthfuls for him. Next morning he was feeling a little stronger. With all my doghood I called upon my nose, and *by the cat's whiskers*, folks, before long if I didn't flush a flock of wild turkeys! A fine moment—that! I can feel my joy this minute." Ippy's tail thumped the earth.

With a sudden foolish squawk the little old hen flew to a low-hanging branch. There she perched, ruffling her feathers. "Speaking of turkeys, once I hovered a brood," she boasted. "But, *pshaw*, I had no real affection for such foreign high-flyers, after I discovered they weren't a hen's proper chickens. Nor did I grieve when two of them flew away forever, and three were caught by the foxes. However, I can fly, as you observe, Friend Appleseed."

"Never mind, Chickabid," chided Johnny, gently. "This is Ippy's hour, and he's arrived at a dramatical moment."

"Now, in haste and excitement," proceeded Ippy, "Jervis aimed at the largest turkey. He missed. Up and away

it flew, likewise the rest of the flock. *The dogberries!*"
whimpered Ippy. "Usually Jervis Cutler was a fine shot,
and his gun and his dog and his love of hunting the breath
of life to him. Now he was weak from hunger. His burns
pained him. Down the poor fellow dropped to a log.
Water ran out of his eyes. Sad, broken sounds came from
his throat. I licked his wet cheeks, trying to comfort
him.

"At that he looked up, and saw one lone turkey perched
on a topmost limb. Very carefully now he wiped his gun.
Slowly he reloaded. Carefully he sighted. *Bang!* Down
turkey tumbled. I ran to retrieve it. How we laughed and
barked! While the bird roasted, how we drooled! *By the
Dog Star*, Johnny, those were the juiciest bones ever I fed
upon! And it wasn't an hour later 'til Jervis killed a deer."

"Help!" cried the little fawn, all of a tremble. "Oh,
where is my doe-mother?"

"Don't be afraid, pet," whispered Megan into the fawn's
ear. "I am your mother."

Ippy lowered his voice. Age had made him gentle.
"Master made a sack of the skin," he continued. "Into it
he put the choicest meat. We went on, capering and barking and whistling. Youth and a full stomach—ah-h!" Ippy
wheezed.

"You're getting tired, old fellow," warned Johnny,
patting him. "Come to the end of the story."

"At last we reached the surveyors' camp we'd left two

weeks before," panted Ippy. "Ashes were still smoking in the stump of a sugar tree, but the party had gone on. Oh, but Master was downcast. I knew it. But the scent of the surveyors' heels lay faint on the earth for me, and for Jervis the men had blazed a trail. Eight more days, during which we had rain, which silenced the leaves underfoot, so that we found plenty of game. At last we came up with the party. And there was Benoni's dog and Jervis's—meaning me—leaping over one another with joy. And how the men shouted, and clapped Jervis on the shoulder! They had thought us dead." Ippy got up stiffly, and stretched.

"A fine story, Ippy," Johnny complimented him, "and a good part you played in it. Andrew!" he called. "You didn't know I'd be adding a dog's tale to my story bag."

"Dog's tail. Ippy. Johnny Appleseed," murmured Andrew. He sat up, rubbing the sleep out of his eyes as Johnny walked past.

At the cabin door the elder McIlvains sat talking. "Look at that bree-gade coming!" whispered the wife, laughing a little. "First comes that odd Johnny-fellow, with Ippy sniffing at his fingers. On yon side the fawn nuzzles Johnny's other hand. Then—I do declare—our Megan, walking light and careful as if she were sleep-walking. And Pa—my old hen, for lawzy's sakes—she, too, must be witched. It's not pure chance she steps so high in Johnny's wake."

"There's Andrew following," Pa muttered. "He's got

dream in 'is eyes again. *Drat,* I thought the United States mail would've cured 'im!'"

"That bree-gade means more'n it appears to mean," murmured Mistress McIlvain, perplexed. "Pa—I—I've heard that Johnny Appleseed and the creatures talk together."

"Shucks!" exclaimed Pa. "Any but a notionatin' body can figger it out." Pa ticked off his arguments on spread fingers. "Johnny's a queer duck, ain't he? He spends most of 'is time in the woods, where the creatures live. With all the dangers, he comes out safe and whole. Yet he never carries a gun, does he? Nor eats a bite of meat. He brings to the cabins unusual gifts, like apple seeds. He brings news from heaven, as if he'd been there yestidday and would be going back for more news tomorrow. That's somehow uncommon comforting. Folks think a sight of him. But do they make 'im out? No, he puzzles 'em. So they begin to think outlandish things about 'im. First thing you know it's talk, and spreading. There's nobody got so long and loose a tongue as a lonesome backwoods settler. Johnny!"

Pa shouted the name almost angrily, and so loud that the hen went half-flying toward the barn. The fawn halted, teetering on its fragile legs. Ippy bit viciously at a flea in his groin. One would never have guessed him to be a historical dog.

"Johnny," repeated Pa, his voice natural and matter-of-fact again. "Got enough seeds in your poke to spare me some? I'll made a dicker with you."

"No dickering needed," answered Johnny, smiling. "Tomorrow I'll grub you out a little plot along the bottoms. Next spring you can sow the seeds. If they were saplings they'd be worth a fi'-penny bit, if you had it. But the seeds I'll exchange for your good will and a bit of salt and maybe a measure of meal for my mush pot."

"We shall have apples?" asked Megan, her dark eyes alight. "What color? What kind?"

"Don't break in, lass," her pa said. "Remember—seen and not heard for your age." He relented. "We don't know what kind 'til they hang from the bough. Apples don't run true to seed."

"But whatever kind they turn out to be, Megan," said Johnny, "they'll give you ripened pleasure. *Comfort me with apples*, so the Good Book says." Exaltation brightened the hollows of Johnny's cheeks.

Andrew edged closer. He'd like to ask Johnny, low-spoken, if he'd heard aright as he lay between the root arms. *Faugh*, a dog can't talk! Had the sound been only that of creek water, rippling like words through the drowsy afternoon? Or had Andrew been actually asleep, and a hunting story Mr. Cutler had once told him come alive again in a dream? Andrew stole a look at Pa. No, he couldn't ask Johnny, not with Pa there; not with Monday, Tuesday and Wednesday written on Pa's face as plain as every day. And ahead of Andrew, were there not many work days of carrying the United States mail, and a long grim gun for defending it? Andrew's eyes turned toward his mother. She smiled at him.

"I've heard," she began softly (for *she* didn't seem to mind Pa's Mondays and Tuesdays), "I've heard how, when the Kentuckians came with their seeds and their thirty plows to clear land and plant a crop for the first settlers at Station Prairie, they found a great ring of wild fruit trees fringing those untouched meadows—haw and plum and crab and mulberry. Must've been a pretty sight that first spring, all white blossom and sweet smell around the brown plowed ground."

"T'would've been a miracle to see, and 'til then no white man a-needing of them," said Johnny. "But you take apples—" He broke off, as his eyes met Andrew's. "Did you ever think, lad, about the names of things? None but a dreamer could've thought up such fair names for apples as *Mountain Sweet* and *Lady Finger*. None but a notionatin' sort could've contrived *Nonesuch* and *French Paradise* and *Favorite*."

"Sabbath or no, Andrew," interrupted Pa, shortly, "there's the bossy to milk."

"Yes, Pa," agreed Andrew. He started to whistle for his dog. But no, let Ippy rest. He'd had a hard afternoon, hadn't he, telling his old-time history to Johnny Appleseed?

1807

FAVORITE

"LITTLE Persis, are you middlin' glad the captain fetched you out to Ohio?" asked half-brother Johnny.

Persis smiled. She knew she was Johnny's favorite among their father's "second batch," as Captain Chapman himself called the brood born to him and Lucy Cooley, the girl he'd married after Johnny's mother died. Persis knew it pleased Johnny to think of her as yet a child, although she was now a sturdy fourteen. Oh, yes, she assured him, she'd liefer live in Ohio than back in Massachusetts. She did not add that, in this winter of 1807, in the family cabin on Duck Creek, she was both happy and sad.

Happiness often springs from very simple things. Persis was happy simply because her youthful prettiness was in full bud. To a girl her own prettiness is like music. It plays its private little tune to her, soothing yet gay, and the tune never ceases so long as the prettiness lasts. Persis was happy because she was finished and done with the tiresome *a,b,c's* of her childhood. She didn't care if she never looked into another book in all her born days. Now she was free to dream and plan, to spin and weave, making the blankets and quilts for her future dowry, as every girl did. She was free to rowdy with the many Chapman cousins who lived at Whipple's Run and along the forks of the creek. There was skating in winter. There were weddings, quiltings and apple-parings, sugar-makings, houseraisings, and sometimes a shoutin' camp-meeting. Such come-togethers made everyone feel *oops-a-daisy*.

Occasionally Persis went with her brothers and cousins when they paddled down to Marietta to trade their furs and corn and pork, and the ginseng they'd gathered on the hills. She'd seen the river traffic there, the crowds around the land office, and some of the fine folk who lived in the town. Once, because she'd heard so much about the Blennerhassetts, Persis had instantly recognized Madame, in her rich clothes and with her Negro attendant, up for a bit of shopping from her island home downriver. *Hey, nonny,* but there was a gracious fine lady! Now, poor Madame Blennerhassett and her Irish aristocrat of a husband had fled away in disgrace, dupes of the scheming Aaron Burr. The fabulous furnishings of the Blennerhassett mansion, set like a jewel amidst its island groves, had been destroyed by drunken soldiers. *Hey nonny no,* the scandal was still the talk of the river country. Although she was sorry for Madame, Persis did adore a bit of gossip.

Persis was happy because she had room to breathe in

this new Ohio cabin. When she thought of that tiny crowded house back in Longmeadow! But now, of course, the eldest of the "second batch" had flown the nest. Indeed, brother Nathanael had been the first to follow Johnny's advice to move West. And up to a few weeks ago, Captain Chapman was fond of razzing brother Perley about how he had begun to *ogle* Carl Ogle's daughter Mary. Looked as if there'd be a wedding one of these days. Pretty soon only the youngest would be left in the Chapman cabin. "Time flies," observed the captain, as if he'd just discovered the fact, and found it both surprising and sad.

But then the captain was scarcely himself since the turn of the year. He lay in his bed day and night. The Chapman cousins declared he wouldn't get well until maple molasses time. Seemed like in this country when the household stock of maple sugar ran out, around August, there was apt to be sickness; and no chirking up until the new sweetenin' smoothed the tongues of the poorly, come February. Wasn't it but natural, folks asked, that the living sap of the sugar trees should impart life-giving strength to a human mortal?

However, Cousin Levi said if it kept up like this, warm and wet, there wouldn't be the freeze-and-thaw needed for a good sugaring off. "Could be," he said, "that Captain has the Duck Creek fever that seems to come from high waters and the mud that never dries. Looks to me," added

Cousin Levi, behind his hand, "that only the Lord Almighty can save the Captain, less'n it might be Doc' Jabez True."

So half-brother Johnny fetched Doctor True, although the fetching was a day's work. It's likely they talked of *Summer Sweetings* and *Favorites* and *Northern Spies* all the way, for they'd known and liked one another as apple-growers for several years. The doctor was an old-fashioned man. He wore knee breeches. His hair was tied back with a ribbon. His manners were graced with a fine, old-fashioned courtesy.

After he'd chatted cheerfully with the captain, and bled him and sweated him and left some powders, Doctor True talked in low tones with Lucy outside the cabin, where the captain couldn't hear him. When he and Johnny set out again for Marietta, Lucy slipped into the loom house and closed the door. Had its heavy timbers been transparent, Persis might have seen her mother sink to the weaver's bench and lean her forehead against the cloth beam. She stayed there for as much as fifteen minutes. When she came out, calm, and saying never a word, there was something gone from her face. The children, young as they were, knew that it was hope, and that in the loom house their mother had said farewell to her life with Captain Chapman.

So this was why Persis, in the midst of her natural youthful joy, was also sad. The shadows that darkened the family cabin were heavier than those of the cloudy winter. It was a blessing, though, that half-brother Johnny could be there. He took over most of the nursing, as gently as a woman. He was so calm and cheerful, and spoke of heaven with such a lovely persuasion that it began to seem as if the captain were merely making ready to journey to a pleasant near-by country, and maybe there was nothing really sad about it, after all. While the captain had always been exceptionally fond of Johnny, he'd never quite approved of the latter's mystical religion. But now he took great comfort in everything that Johnny said. "Let him worship as he pleases," the captain recommended. "It's a free country," a thing that Americans had been saying with certainty since 1782, and would say, as long as it remained true. These days the captain could scarcely bear to have Johnny out of his sight, and when he wasn't too weak and feverish, he enjoyed Johnny's talk of the new lands as much as did the children. Johnny told more of himself than was his wont, for it is natural that a father should wish to hear what his son has been doing, and the captain hadn't much breath left for asking questions.

"When I went back to the border after seeds, in the fall of 1805," said Johnny, "I was set on bringing enough to do me a while, for I aimed to plant more plots than ever before, and in farther country. So I busied myself around the cider mills, sorting out the plumpest and brightest seeds. I visited my old friends. It's great country for holdin' forth on religion, there being every kind and creed. Many a time we'd argufy 'til the small hours, and then not done. There's Jefferson County, too, a region of old Indian fighters—mighty men who are still obliged to tuck their fists into their armpits to keep from shooting any Indian they happen to lay eyes on. The stories those old giants can tell curdle the blood.... Well, I called on my friend Judge Young up in Greensburg, in Pennsylvania, and got me a new supply of tracts. I reached Metzger's on the Youghiogheny in time to see Nancy married. Doesn't seem possible the child's old enough to be tidying a cabin of her own in Ohio, at New Philadelphia.... I beat along the Virginia side to Jacob Neisley's, and like to've popped my eyes out with the sight of his far-spread acres of fruit trees. Distills his own brandy and ships it down to the mouth of the Mississippi by the raft-loads. But I couldn't take ary one of Neisley's seeds—not the way I feel 'bout grafting. For Jacob grafts, and it's against God's master plan.

"Well, at the land office in Steubenville I bought a plot of my own a few miles below that village. Come spring of 1806, I planted there. Then I got a couple of canoes and lashed 'em together and loaded them with the bags of seeds I'd collected. Any settlers who happened to see me coming down the Ohio called out to know what I'd got, and some of 'em mighty sorrowful to hear it wasn't cloth or kettles, hand-mills or tools. But for them that set store by apples and welcomed me, I climbed ashore and planted.

"I stopped here to see you folks, you remember, and then I went up the Muskingum to Coshocton and branched off along the Mohican. I planted sixteen bushels of seed on the Walhonding. New as creation is that wild land, and hardly anybody there but white traders and Indians."

"Tell us something exciting," suddenly clamored seven-year-old Davis.

"Below Newark the Licking River flows through a deep gorge," said Johnny. "Black as pitch is that river, and moves without a sound. The very shadows there are ebony. The trees are of night darkness—hemlock and spruce, with never a bird in them, nor scarce a stir of branches. It's like as if a great hand of silence hung over the place. And there *is* a hand there! Gave me a queer turn when first I saw it. Seemed 'twas ready to reach out and grab me."

"What was it?" cried young Jonathan Cooley, his cheeks pale.

"It's a great hand chiseled out on the wall of the gorge by long-ago Indians, so 'tis said. Fingers and thumb point east," Johnny explained. "Time, or some dark mossy growth has blackened it, and given that lone place its name—the *Black Hand Narrows*. The Indians won't go nigh, if they can help, but once persuaded they whisper strange stories about it."

"I'd rather hear of people," declared Persis, shivering.

"Been carrying around a story this long while, little

Persis," Johnny volunteered, obligingly. "Had it direct from Missus Phinehas Ford.

"The Fords pioneered from Pennsylvania to Marietta early in 1799, and in May, with their two babies, they loaded their goods on a flatboat and took to the Ohio. The John Joneses were with them, Lilly Jones being own sister to Mistress Ford. At the mouth of the Scioto they began poling up to where some old Pennsylvania neighbors of theirs had settled, near a great circle of Indian mounds. There they wintered until about tree-tapping season, when the Joneses farewelled, going on to the place they had in mind, on Raccoon Creek. Greenup time came. The Fords went upriver and reached Franklinton 'bout the last o' May. 'Twas then little more than a clearing in unbroken wilderness. Phinehas got a wagon and team of oxen. One day, with his little family, he set out through the woods for Auter Creek, a branch of the Licking, where he'd laid out in 'is mind to build a grist mill.

"Mis' Ford told me their journey couldn't've been more beset with trouble if the oxen'd been shod with bad luck itself. At best 'twas hard going. But one day they came to a run of water. The oxen were going down its steep bank, bracing themselves 'gainst the push of the wagon, when a great dangling grapevine caught under the yoke. Swung those poor critters right off their feet." Johnny gave his one suspender a humorous hitch while his young half brothers snickered. "The critters hung helpless, their feet

pawing—nothing," Johnny continued. "Of course Phinehas cut the vine, but fell into the water in the doing of it.
The animals floundered a-plenty, and Missus Ford and her
little Hannah had to cling to the wagon seat for dear life.

"That safely over, one of the wagon wheels split. Took
a whole day for Phinehas to mend it, there in the wild
woods. Next day if he didn't break the stock of 'is gun,
saving the wagon from turning over. Trouble was,"
chuckled Johnny, "that piece of woods just didn't give
room for a wagon and team.

"But at last they reached Auter Creek. Phinehas put up
a little bark-covered cabin. Wife called it snug, and what
did the babes care if there wasn't another mortal within
five miles? And five miles amid forest so dense are twice as
long as a surveyor's miles.

"It was too late to plant a corn crop. The Fords had
eaten up their garden stuff, 'cept some punkins. The stock
of staples they'd brought by wagon was running low.
'Wife,' declared Phinehas, 'if we're to live and breathe in
the backwoods, I must take the team back to Franklinton
for food.'

" 'And before the fall rains set in,' agreed the missus.
She hid the sudden shaking of her hands under her apron,
for she couldn't help remembering how the wolves howled
around the cabin the nights through, and many's the time
she'd heard the scratch of a panther's claws on the roof.

"One morning Phinehas set out. He'd be back within

six days, God willing. Then—well, he and the team might as well've been chipmunks, the way the trees gathered 'em in and closed up after 'em. At first it didn't seem too bad for Missus Ford. The babies' prattle and the purr of the hearth fire was comforting. She had the extra gun. The provisions would last, with care, until Phinehas returned.

"But about the third day it seemed to get uncommon lonesome, for no reason, maybe, 'cept time was stretching out. The fifth day the wolves that up to now prowled in the clearing only at night, began to linger through the day. They ran when Missus fired her gun, but through the chinks of the door that Phinehas had made by interlacing small poles with hickory bark, she could see the beasts' eyes gleaming from among the tree trunks. When she was obliged to go to the spring for fresh water, she must gather up her courage and put it on as 'twere a cloak of nettles. She'd leave a pine knot burning on the doorstone to keep the wolves away. 'Twasn't easy, carrying the heavy gun and the loaded water-pail yoke up the hill.

"In the long and lonely days and the restless nights Missus Ford wondered how the wolves knew she was alone and a woman. There was one in p'ticular, uglier than the rest, bolder. He was always there, tongue out and dripping. To the woman his face became the very face of evil, a savage evil that knows and bides its time.

"Rain began to fall. The woman's store of powder became too damp for firing the gun. And didn't that make her feel helpless? She prayed to God with all her power. The next night it poured in torrents. In the morning the wolves were gone, even the ugly one. Somewhere, away from the rain, they lay snug in their dens. Phinehas's wife breathed easier.

"The seventh day came, and the eighth. Rain drummed on the roof, hour after hour. Loneliness was a live thing caged within the cabin, dogging her every step. The stock of food dwindled to almost nothing. The ninth day. No Phinehas. Injured and alone in the woods? Worse, maybe. Or was he only held up by high waters? There were no bridges, and whenever the rain slackened, Missus Ford could hear the roaring of the creek.

"Well, she must leave the cabin. Before the food ran out, while the rain held off the wolves, she must make her way through the forest to her sister Lilly's, five miles distant. She rigged up a holder for strapping baby Margaret to her back. She scalded the last bit of meal, and made bread to take along.

"The tenth day crep' in without rain, but veiled with fog. All day she waited. That night the wolves came back, but before dawn rain was again falling. When the woman looked out, the beasts were gone. She hurried from the cabin with her children. Around her the forest dropped its dark curtain of solitude and unknown dangers.

"It took Missus Ford six hours to travel those five miles. She had to choose her steps one by one over the spreading roots and through the wet bracken. The burden of the children often forced her to stop and rest. That journey was a nightmare that still haunts her. But at last, drenched and weary and sobbing, she saw before her the Jones's cabin. In the clearing stood Phinehas's wagon. He had only just arrived. By next evening the Fords were back in their own hut on Auter Creek."

"Did Phinehas build his mill?" asked the captain.

"Yes," answered Johnny. "When there's water enough to turn the wheel, the settlers gather there by the dozen, waiting to get their grain ground. Often they stay all night, so far they come. But it's little sleeping they do. Talk, talk, talk! Why," laughed Johnny, "I've heard 'em settle all the problems of mankind in one night's gabbing. They buy Louisiana over again, but at a lower price. They go with Zebulon Pike to the far West. They rip Napoleon up the back and they praise Thomas Jefferson. 'Is there any good Indian but a dead one?' they ask.... 'It's cheaper, ain't it,' they argue, 'to boil down your own salt, however far you must go to reach a lick, than 'tis to trade your four good buckskins, or your fine large bear pelt, or your sixteen 'coon skins for a paltry fifty pounds of it?' ... 'Is there anything tastier than bears' feet roasted in hot ashes?' 'Yes, there's beaver's tail, an' there's buffalo's tongue.' For the rest of the night the men out-talk one another with tales of hunting and trapping.... Well, Phinehas Ford has a fine young orchard soon to bear fruit. He claims to have started the first apple orchard in his county. Catherine Stadden claims the same glory. One way or t'other, I don't take sides," laughed Johnny.

February on Duck Creek brought a welcome change of weather. Night wore a frill of ice on its garments, day a sheen of pale sunlight. In the sugar bush the fragrant sap dripped through hand-whittled spiles into pails. The great iron kettles were hung and filled, the fires lighted and the boiling done. Then, soaked with thick golden sirup, did not the everyday mush and pone become food fit for gods?

But the sweetenin' came too late to hearten Captain Chapman. He was at deadly grips with the chills-and-fever. In burning dreams he wandered into the past. He was little orphan Nate again, living with his uncle Davis on an old New England farm. He was back in Leominster. Wife Lucy seemed to become Elizabeth Simonds, a girl Nathanael had loved and lost. Sometimes, in the firelight, the face of General Washington flickered on the cabin wall. Once, when it became fixed, and clear-cut as a coin engraving, the captain half-rose from his pillow, trying to sing some long-remembered words. When he failed, Johnny took them up, clear and strong, while the captain sank back, content:

> The day is broke, my boys, push on
> And follow, follow Washington,
> 'Tis he that leads the way,
> 'Tis he that leads the way,

"Follow, follow Washington"—these were the last words spoken by Captain Chapman before he died on February 18th, in the sixty-first year of his age. For in brave and bitter days of long ago, when there was none better to follow than General George Washington, nor any half so great, Nathanael Chapman had been a young "Continentaler."

Kin and neighbors gathered. There was mourning. But Johnny said not to grieve. He said the captain's life and his rebirth into heaven was like the growth of seed to tree, and to flower, and to fruit. "That is God's Nature-plan," declared Johnny, "as wonder-working and natural for men and angels as for any earth-growing thing."

Johnny said he must be going on to his work. "You'd best settle down with us and mind your future," urged his half brothers. "We'll have orchards here, but we'll sell, not give. John, you'll be poor all your life," they warned him.

"I sow," answered Johnny, quietly, "and some day I'll reap. Treasures in heaven. Apples of gold."

As he turned away, they stared at him, not understanding. Lucy spoke for him. "When Johnny was a little tad in Longmeadow I used to fuss at making him over, so he'd be more like other folks," she said. "Now he's thirty-three, well—I never thought to see him half so queer. Look at those strange eyes, and that long untrimmed hair and those poor duds. All the same, he's been heart-comforting to me, and he's got a tongue in his head as good as any preacher. Your father told me you're not to fault Johnny for the kind he is. He's religious like his own ma, only Johnny— he's possessed by it. One day your father said to me, after he'd lain studyin' in his mind, 'Lu, aren't apple seeds *faith?* Then, isn't it pure faith my son John plants in the wilderness?' "

Persis remembered that years later, when some writing fellow came asking questions of her. For it was not until after Johnny had gathered his "apples of gold" in heavenly orchards that the realization of Johnny's legend dawned upon her. Then she knew that her half brother, John Chapman, and the queer, beloved Johnny Appleseed were identical yet separate, the one gone from earth, the other living on.

"Good-by, folks," said Johnny, that February of 1807. "Look out for any marauding Indians. They may never come this far for attack, but there's danger brewing. I smell it on the wind. Farewell, little Persis, farewell."

"Little Persis," and she nearly fifteen! Gentle, amusing Johnny!

1812

NORTHERN SPY

ZACK MILLER's hand moved out from his side as stealthily as a field mouse moves among the grasses. In the dark his fingers found and rested upon his musket, affectionately. Since he'd been knee-high to a 'hopper, adventure and a gun had been his boon companions, whether he'd hunted for bear or elk, deer or 'coon. Or, as at present, for plain ornery Injun.

Zack, at eighteen, was the youngest of the four government scouts on this beat. He could make out the shadow that was Captain Downing only because he knew it was there, the motionless sentinel shadow of the first night watch, at the big oak on the knoll above Conotton Creek. John Cuppy and Jim Foulks lay each within a thirty pace radius of Zack and the tree, but so still, so wrapped in darkness as to be invisible.

Zack had not been scouting for the government long. He liked the danger and responsibility, the pride in serving because of his daring, his woods wisdom, his superb marksmanship. Of course he would rather be hunting for game, especially this time of year, when bears fed on the mast wherever there were beeches; when the turkeys were so juicy and fat; when the skin of the deer was prime. On hunting trips Zack could have his dog with him. For a moment the smooth bore of the gun under Zack's hand became the satin smooth head of Bose, his little ol' coon-dog back in Virginny. Likely Bose was howling throat-deep for Zack these nights.

But this was the autumn of 1812, a time of war. No hunting for pleasure, but a bunch of scouts tracking out savages in this northern Ohio country. Tuscarawas country in a high backbone, the stream to the west of it flowing westward, those to the east seeking the Ohio. Wild country, very sparsely settled. To the bigwigs in Washington and to the brave little ships on sea and lakes, war meant America against England. But the enemy of the frontiersman was the terrible red man. If there could have been a few more victories like that of General Harrison at Tippecanoe last year, out in Indiana Territory! But God himself had set His warning in the sky of coming terror. *Napoleon's Comet*, the blazing streak was called in some parts of the world, but here folks had called it *Tecumseh's Comet*. And hadn't there also been a series of earthquakes last winter, the bluffs along the Ohio crumbling, and the course of streams in the Mississippi valley being changed in a mad, crazy way? Dreadful portents, these, coming true now in panic and disaster. Only last month General Hull had surrendered Fort Detroit to the British, and the yelling Indians were running amok throughout the frontier. Zack had heard of the recent tragedy at Checagou, the savages pouncing from behind the golden sand dunes to tomahawk the men, women and children who were vacating Fort Dearborn. *Drat* Hull, what Americans were saying about him was not fit to repeat before ladies! Yet Zack himself didn't know too much about the war. He'd attend to his little part in it, and woe betide the Injun who came within range of his gun!

Lying in the dark, Zack could smell the perfume of ripe grapes. He couldn't have named it, but somehow it was poetry; it was beauty festooning the night. But *pshaw*, he wasn't used to such soft fancies! He turned restlessly on his blanket. *Hang it*, what had come over him since leaving Fort Henry that he couldn't drop off to sleep as readily as a cub fox by its mother? . . . *It's that apple! It's that dratted apple she gave me. Why don't I take it out of my blouse and eat it and be rid of it?*

Zack Miller, then you wouldn't have it any more! Besides, a hearty fellow can't eat a good juicy apple 'thout making a noise like a horse. A creepin' Injun might hear a gov'ment spy a-horsing an apple given him by a girl he'd never dreamed had ever looked at him, 'til she up and chose him to say good-by to with an apple. A pink-stripedy apple, mighty pretty. What's pretty—the apple or the girl? Oh, she's sweet as a bee-tree full of honey . . .

But what made 'er do it, all of a sudden like that, and s'prise
me and trouble me ever since, tryin' to think of somethin'
kinda nice I might've said, if ever I could've?

Zack saw again the September morning at Wheeling,
the villagers gathered at the fort to bid the scouts God-
speed, and to show their trust in men hand-picked for
ranging the wilderness in advance of the regiment. The
fort chaplain had offered prayer. The commandant made
a little speech. There were tears. But there was rough banter too, the girls, with posies in their hair, giving their
kisses to the bachelor scouts because of the incredible peril
that lay ahead. Zack hung back. He was bashful of girls.

And then, of a sudden, this little Molly Campbell was
holding out an apple to Zack. Shy she was, her cheeks like
fire-pinks, her eyes blue as day-flowers. "Here," she said,
"it's for you." And when he took the apple and turned
away, red as all-get-out, and with never a word of thanks
—*idiot!*—she had added, softly, "Be sure to come back
safe, Isaac." 'Stead of ol' everyday Zack—*Isaac!* On Molly
Campbell's lips his name had been as sweet and mysterious
as a whisper of dawn wind in summer. *Now—whatever*
made 'er—...hold on, there, don't start that rigmarole
again! Before he knew it, would come his turn as sentinel.
Was an apple to scatter the wits and upset the habits of a
crack government spy? Grimly Zack began touching and
naming his equipment. From his belt at the right hung his
tomahawk: left, his hunting-knife in its leather sheath; his

bullet bag. The gun lay at hand. He was fully dressed. Within the overlap of his shirt was his corn pone, his jerk, and a bit of tow for cleaning his gun. The apple—*bosh!* Presently Zack fell asleep.

About midnight Cuppy, standing second watch, saw a crawling body. He cocked his gun. Instantly that slow-creeping motion froze. Instantly also the three sleeping scouts, trained to waken at the slightest sound, seized their arms and crept toward the oak. The body moved again. Cuppy fired. It lay still, but they put no trust in it. Cautiously Foulks crawled toward it and hurled his tomahawk. For minutes the scouts waited. Finally Foulks examined the body. It was that of a wolf. Both shot and tomahawk had pierced its brain. For fear the report of the gun had advised any skulking Indians of their location, the scouts moved a quarter of a mile upstream. Now Zack stood watch. Nothing happened. Only the bright host of stars marched across the sky. No sound save the liquid whisper of water, the faint brush of velvety owl-wing aslant the silent air, a nut dropping to earth. At dawn, after exploring the region, the men dared to start a blaze for breakfast. Wiping out all trace of their camp, two of them went back and buried the wolf, covering the spot with leaves. The day was young when the four trod single-file toward the headwaters of Conotton Creek. Not a moccasin print did they leave behind them.

There followed two days of marching northward

through uninhabited country. The weather was as mellow as the apple in Zack's shirt. Every bough was a bright October banner. The alders and the woodbine hung out their clusters of berries, scarlet and purple. The haze among the trees was smoky-blue, like the autumn coat of the deer. Birds lingered in soft-hued flocks, southward bound. Zack felt gloriously alive. His craving to meet and outsmart danger was as keen as the blade of his hunting knife.

About sunset the following day the scouts approached "Indian Camp," so-called because old trails converged where once the red men had set up their hunting lodges. It was now a place of brambles and coarse grass. Two thorny old apple trees bore on their trunks the nesting holes of screech owls.

Jim Foulks, in the lead, suddenly halted and gave warning. "Hist!" Instantly the others took to the thickets, their muskets readied. Among the trees of Indian Camp they saw a flutter of rags, a flick and toss of long dark hair. No Indian that, unless the ghost of a squaw.

"Halt!" cried Foulks, shadowing the ghost with his gun. A pair of naked brown legs vanished behind a tree. After a moment their owner peered out. The eyes in that face, even from this distance, were strangely brilliant. Now a man stepped forth. He held up his calloused palms in surrender, standing silent and unafraid as the scouts advanced.

Foulks tossed a chuckle backward as he shouldered his

gun. "I've seen this bird before," he said, out of the corner of his mouth. "He's about as dangerous as a beaker of milk. ...Anybody here but you, Battle-ax?" he asked roughly.

"My name is John Chapman," stated the other, and although the tatters that scarcely covered him gave him the look of a beggar, his words were clothed with dignity. "Better known, perhaps, as Johnny Appleseed," he explained. "You're welcome to my cooking fire."

" 'Twill save us the time of starting one, and much obliged!" Captain Downing responded. There were no other introductions. Spies do not name their own. Cuppy cleaned and fried some fish. The scouts were low on food. Johnny, who had already eaten his mush and washed his kettle, offered the men hazel nuts from a small hoard. He withdrew to one of the old apple trees, seating himself at its foot, cracking nuts with his teeth. He paid the spies little attention. It was almost as if they weren't there. But when they had finished their meal, he rose up and shook the tree. The sound of the dozen or so little apples falling to earth gave Zack a boyish notion to help pick them up. As he did so, he noticed Johnny Appleseed straighten, sniffing curiously. "I smell a better apple than these," he declared. Zack said nothing. What kind of a wildling was Johnny, that he could smell out the hidden fruit in Zack's shirt-bosom?

The little Indian apples were divided. They were scarcely worth the eating, but their dry tartness lay pleasantly on the tongue. Their bright color was a bit of cheer in the dusky wood. Now the embers of the fire were covered. The light drained out of the sky.... "A better apple," mused Zack. *Oh yes, it was a wonderful apple—an apple of farewell passing from a girl's soft giving hand to the hand of a boy.* But the last time Zack had dared to peep at it, the skin, once so firm and polished, was wrinkling. He'd either have to eat it, or—*Botheration,* how it troubled him! Yet how his mind loved to dwell on it! *Now, whatever made 'er—*

The captain was asking questions of Johnny Appleseed. Zack hitched closer, straining to hear. For on their beat the scouts allowed their talk to rest on the air no heavier than thistledown, whether it was of nothings, or about such vital matters as the new national pike, recently begun in Virginia. "You been around this country a while?" Zack heard the captain ask.

"All around," answered Johnny. "Wonderful country for apples. Three year ago I bought a little acreage of Alexander Finley near Tylerstown and to Joseph Walker I gave fifty dollars for a strip at Mount Vernon. I've got me a good nursery near Mifflin. I built me a cabin at Caleb Palmer's near New Haven. Sometimes, in the marshes of that country, I pick cranberries and I sell 'em. The region right round here has fewer people. But I been all over," declared Johnny. "Moons ago I planted an orchard on Indian Fork. Peter Bohard, first settler there, aims to lay out a town when 'nough folks come. Says my orchard will draw 'em like wild cherries draw the birds." In the dusk Johnny's face was only a shape. But as he spoke of his orchard Zack somehow knew that his eyes were smiling. "Been 'way down on the Elkhorn to transplant some saplings," Johnny went on. "The settlers in this part of Ohio'd just begun to trickle in when the trouble started." *Trouble* —it was a heavy word, coming from Johnny.

"Seen any Indians?" asked the captain. "Know anything?"

"Haven't seen any Indians since I left the Huron and Mohican country, but you'll be meeting them," Johnny asserted. "Far as knowing anything, I know plenty. Harrison's ordered even the friendly Indian villages broken up. So the Jeromeville Indians were placed under American protection at Urbana. But who's going to answer for the taking of the Indian wife and daughter of Trader Baptiste Jerome, and left him forsaken? And there's the Indians at Greentown, promising they'd make no trouble, if only they might stay in their village. But the military came to James Copus, because he'd preached to the Greentown folk and was their friend, asking him to persuade the Indians to leave. 'Say to them,' said the white officer, 'that their huts and possessions will be protected until their return.' But hardly had the Indians set off for Mansfield, when the white guards put Greentown to the torch. Set hate afire, too. So there's been butchery on the Black Fork.

James Copus is no more, and dead are the soldiers who were guarding his cabin. Martin Ruffner—alas, I knew him well, a big, bold fellow who hated all Indians. He'd gone to warn the Zimmers. The Indians came. Ruffner died hard, and fighting. The Zimmers were killed and scalped. Oh, there's trouble," sighed Johnny, "and there'll be more. Friends," he warned, "when you sleep, sleep lightly."

But the night could not have been more peaceful had the scouts been at Fort Henry, ringed about with guards. Zack stood the last watch, and at dawn saw the strange apple-planter strip and bathe in the nearby stream. Having dried himself with bunches of grass, he donned his tatters as carefully as if they had been linen and broadcloth. He combed out his long locks. *If he'd fix himself up the fellow wouldn't be bad looking*, thought Zack. He looked away when Johnny knelt in silent prayer. It was not a time for spying on a man.

Cuppy and Foulks made the usual reconnoiter before breakfast. The meal was scant indeed. "Bet you a fi'penny bit I kill us a deer today," joked Zack.

But before anyone could take the wager, Johnny Appleseed spoke up. "The report of a gun will bring the Indians a-swarming out of their hidings."

"You prophesied us attackted and scalped las' night," muttered Foulks, "yet we slept like babes."

"I can smell danger from afar," declared Johnny. "It

comes to me now, dark and bitter as smoke."

"Pugh!" mocked Foulks. "Bet you smell Zack's apple. He's been carryin' it so love-precious it must be far gone with rot." Foulks flashed an impish grin at Zack.

The boy felt the red creep up his neck. *Plague-gone* Jim Foulks! Then he'd seen Molly Campbell hand out the apple at Fort Henry that day. Zack got up, pretending it was but rough give-and-take between men. "Just for that," he laughed, "you can wash my dish." He jammed the greasy tin down on Jim's coonskin cap, and strode off into the woods. When he was out of sight, he drew the apple from his shirt. "Love-precious"—eh! Well, it wasn't quite the apple it had once been. With his hunting knife he dug a grave in the earth for Molly Campbell's apple. "Here lies"—in Zack's heart a small ghost seemed to be shedding mourner's tears.

"It's a pity," spoke a voice, so gentle it could have been Molly's own. "Pity not to eat and enjoy a good apple," said Johnny Appleseed. "Leave it here unsavored, and how are you to say for someone's pleasure, when you get home again, that it was the best apple ever you tasted?" Johnny stooped and lifted the apple out of its grave. He polished it on his ragged sleeve and handed it to Zack. The boy split it in two with his thumbs. He gave half to Johnny. They ate in sober silence. "Save the seeds," admonished Johnny, when they had finished. He tore a fragment from his shirt. Carefully he wrapped the seeds.

"Once you get home, plant them, lad," he said. "One or other of them will grow up to be a living memory." They trudged back to rejoin the other men. Johnny gave them directions for reaching Big Sandy Creek. As if Indian Camp were his manor house, and he its host, he spoke his farewells.

The day was fine, decked with October's flaming foliage. At moments when the men forgot their meat-hunger, they felt almost gay. They debated among themselves as to whether they should heed Johnny Appleseed's warning against shooting game. "We're almost at the end of our beat, and no Indians," Cuppy reminded his captain. "Looks to me as if there's none around."

"Might look like Sunday-go-to-meeting, and yet an Injun behind every bush," chuckled Zack.

"And I've heard that Appleseed has close knowledge of the Indians," cautioned Captain Downing. "Some may laugh at his claim of 'smelling danger,' yet it's said he's a wizard at foretelling."

"Nothing more than a backwoods fairy tale," scoffed Foulks. "How could Heaven inspire such a looking creature with the spirit of prophecy? Why, even the Indians think he's crazy, and do him no harm, believing he's under the Great Spirit's special care."

It was Zack who shot the deer that afternoon, as pretty a piece of markmanship as ever brought down a supper. The sun was still high in the west when the scouts reached the Big Sandy and fell to skinning and dressing the deer, of which they made short work. Captain Downing took over the watch. He delegated Foulks to cook the supper. Cuppy was to prepare the sleeping places. Zack must grain the deerskin while it was still warm, and repair the moccasins.

Supper by the Big Sandy was a feast more hearty for hungry men than mush and hazel nuts. The smoke from the campfire soared into the still air, the water rippled below the banks, and the grasses in the lovely savannah beyond were as tall and golden as wheat. One day more, and the turning homeward.... *Could a bashful gawk say to a girl "I ate the apple, and 'twas the best—?" Perhaps he'd have the spunk to tell her he'd saved the seeds for memory's sake....Memory? Maybe he'd get powerful bold and use a sweeter word.* At the thought of such daring, Zack could scarcely swallow. But the meat went down with a quick, hard gulp as the watchword hissed through the air. An instant later the crack of Captain Downing's rifle seemed to split all creation. Beyond Big Sandy an Indian fell dead among the grasses. As he spun, his silver half-moon ornaments danced crazily against his breast.

The scouts, seizing their rifles, scrambled down to the creek in time to see a second brave in flight. Foulks's bullet sent him crashing headlong into the water. Suddenly the hill some distance away sprouted a moving red horde of savages. Their fiendish yells were in imitation of the cries of the forest—the panther's scream, the wolf's long howl, hoot and bray, squawk and wail. "Every man for himself!" shouted Captain Downing. "Scatter! Run for your lives!"

So that was the way of it. Zack lost sight of Cuppy and Foulks as they streaked off in different directions. The Captain disappeared. But Zack stayed on. In the copse by the creek he danced like old Harry's goat, drawing the enemy's fire, dodging their bullets, giving his comrades time to get away. There was a dancing within him, too, and he knew it was the small, quick dancing of fear. But there was also the thrill of defying death, cutting his grisly capers there by the Big Sandy.

He teased the red men as long as he dared. Every second they drew nearer. Suddenly Zack dashed away, zigzagging at first, then launching into long bounding curves. He scarcely touched earth. It was not in vain he'd been the champion foot racer and high jumper back home. Now there were but two, perhaps three Indians in pursuit.

Bounding southward, Zack presently saw Little Fork at its mouth and beyond, a strip of open bottom land overgrown with wild morning-glory and pea vines. His feet went on, but his mind seemed to stop with shock, for he saw that the stream was far too wide to jump. No mortal man could do it. To wade it would slow him, perhaps fatally. A bullet splashed the water. An arrow whistled past his ear.... *Be sure to come back safe, Isaac....* Muscles and will hardened. The curve of his flight broadened into a great leap. Then he was running among the pea vines on the other side, his feet dry. He looked back and beheld one Indian standing at the stream's brink, open-mouthed at something incredible he had seen. Zack had no time to puzzle over the Indian's expression. He turned to fire, then sped on, not knowing whether his shot had found its mark.

But after a while he knew that he ran alone through the falling darkness. Presently, by the North Star, that friend of travelers, he set his course eastward. All night he journeyed. The wheeling planets, the dark, swaying boughs, the shadows pitch-black amid the night glooms, the thud of his own feet, wove a fabric of monotony in his mind. Yet through its dark pattern flashed a silver wonder. *How in the world did I jump that far, and my feet dry? I can't remember—I can't remember. How'd I do it?* Toward dawn he struck Yellow Creek. He followed it to the Ohio, and found the canoe there, hidden and waiting.

The next day the four spies, one by one, straggled lamely into Fort Henry. Downing had a bullet in his arm. Foulks was unharmed. Cuppy told how he'd doubled back. Having gained on his pursuers by this ruse, he had time to build a campfire. Beside it he placed an effigy of himself, wearing his own cap, sleeping under his own blanket. Stationed behind a tree, he saw the two Indians steal up, saw them shoot the false blanketed sleeper, then rush triumphantly to take the scalp. Cuppy fired. One Indian fell, never again to draw breath. The other fled.

So there was breathless listening at the fort, but no celebration, only joy in the warm hand-clasps and on the smiling lips. It took Zack a hesitant while to edge through the crowd and sidle up to Molly Campbell. For a moment he could do nothing but feast his eyes on her face that was lifted to his like a flower to the light. "I met the strange one they call Johnny Appleseed," Zack burst out softly. "He said 'twas a pity not to enjoy a good apple. 'Twas the best ever I ate."

But Molly had no thought just now for Johnny Appleseed, nor for the apple. "You came back safe, Isaac," she breathed, and those sparkles in her eyes were unshed tears.

"I jumped a crick too wide for man or beast to jump, and my feet dry," answered Zack. Because of the tears he dared to speak her name. "Molly, seemed as if I heard you say, there at the crick—" But he couldn't finish, not with so many folks around.

It is written that Zack Miller lived to be a hundred and more, and saw the wonders of progress—the waterways laced with canals, and the rivers bearing queenly steamboats. The wilderness was no more, nor Johnny Appleseed. The Indians vanished: the trails became highways and railroads. The crude settlements grew into towns and cities. But now and then Isaac dreamed back to the old times and saw Johnny Appleseed again, not his tatters, nor his horny bare feet, but kindness itself, making and sharing a little ceremony in the woods with a greenhorn of a lad.

But more often Isaac Miller pondered on how he'd jumped that stream in Carroll County. Deep in his heart he knew it was because a girl had whispered that he must come back to her. But a man doesn't speak aloud of such things. Only the girl herself had been told, for only she would believe it.

1817

FALLAWATER

THIS was the year of the big frost. For years to come the settlers would speak of it with a kind of shocked pride in Nature's dramatic contrariness. "Remember?" they would ask, "after corn-planting in May of '17, how the snow like to have buried us all? And come June, as 'twere November, there fell so heavy a frost as to kill the young fruit and strip the trees of their leaves?"

So this was the cold summer, the fruit killed, and Johnny Appleseed vanished, none knew where. "Why doesn't Uncle Johnny come to see us any more?" fretted the chil-

dren who lived along the Black and Clear Forks, by the
Huron and the Mohican, the Licking and the Sandusky
rivers, by Honey and Switzer and Indian creeks? "Could
Johnny Appleseed be layin' somewhere sick unto death
with the winter plague, cold as it is, and him half-naked?"
fussed the women. "Has he been bit by a massasauga, barefoot as he goes?"... "No rattlesnake could bite through
Johnny's tough hide and live," answered the men, trying
to be reassuring. "That wander-foot of a Johnny will turn
up. He allus does, the blessed ol' coon." But inwardly,
they felt disquieted.

So where was Johnny Appleseed, his young apples
black and shriveled on the branches? Oh, when he'd has-
tened to his orchards and seen the ravages done by the
frost, a hot blend of pain, anger and despair had swept
over him, for he was only human, and his orchards dearer
to him than life. Then God had punished him, or so he
believed, and struck him down in the forest. He thought
his end had come. Lying there, alone and helpless, he
pondered on it, and at first he rejoiced, thinking that in
spite of his sins, he would soon enter that world of eternal
bliss to which he aspired. But the next moment his nurseries seemed to call him, like children bereft. And the
pioneers—why, many a one had never yet laid eyes on an
apple tree in his settlement. Unlike the lower Muskingum
and Ohio country, whose orchards were now producing
tons of fruit, gallons of apple butter, rivers of brandy,

these northern midlands relied almost altogether on
Johnny's young plantings. How could he die, when there
was so much yet to do? He thought of his pioneer friends,
the Palmers and Gladdens and Springers, the Baughmans
and Bartleys and Coulters, the Olivers and Rices and
Masons and many others, who loved him not only for his
services, but for himself. Hadn't they honored him last
year by naming him as the Fourth of July orator? He'd
spoken to a handful of them in Levi Cole's cabin in Nor-
walk. Perhaps, because for some of them it had been their
first Fourth in Ohio, and they a little shaken with home-
sickness and the significance of the day, Levi's cabin had
seemed alight with exaltation, and Franklin and Washington there, Paul Revere and Patrick Henry and the signers
of the Declaration.

Oh, he loved all men, mused Johnny, tenderly, and he
loved all this Ohio land. But these were the folk he loved
best because they had needed him, and this the beloved
country—the Western Reserve; the Firelands; Mansfield
and Ashland and the fertile valleys of the Mohican, the
Walhonding and the Tuscarawas; the Sandusky plains.
He knew almost every inch of it. He knew all the settlers
and the traders, and many of the Indians by name.

Lying prone in his illness, Johnny reviewed his life.
Pictures seemed to hang among the forest boughs above
him, forming and vanishing, one after another. Those
which lingered longest were of the war years, from 1812

to 1815, bitter years for everyone, sad, yet deeply grat-
ifying to Johnny, because his mission had come nearest
to fulfillment. Not only had he tended his nurseries faithfully during the war, but he had ofttimes acted as scout
and messenger for those confined in the blockhouses. Terrible news he had brought of the dark deeds of the
scalp-takers, neighbors massacred and cabins consumed by
flames. Once Johnny had run all night from Mansfield to
Wooster, rousing the frightened settlers on the way, and
returning next morning with a reinforcement of soldiers.
But as the long months passed, he had brought, or shared
joyful news of American victories, at Fort Meigs on the
Maumee, at Fort Stephenson on the Sandusky, Perry's
great victory on Lake Erie, and at last the Battle of the
Thames, where the Indian leader, Tecumseh, was slain,
and Detroit recaptured. How the pioneers cheered the
names of Commander-in-chief William Henry Harrison
and his generals!

Amid Johnny's contemplation of these large events,
many small personal dramas recurred to him—the young
girl walking to the blockhouse through the night's dark
cold without cloak or shoes, but carrying the family treasure, the great Bible: the wife of Johnny's close friend,
Caleb Palmer, tearing down her heavy curtains, improvis-
ing a pair of saddlebags to carry to safety her valuables,
chief of which were two baby daughters: at another time
Johnny and Caleb watching from ambush the burning of

the Palmer cabin, with all the precious grain stored therein: the woman distracted by the loss of her small son, jolted from the wagon the night she and her family fled from their cabin in wild haste. Johnny smiled, as he recalled the boy's restoration.

Johnny remembered the dreadful discomfort and tedium suffered at the blockhouses, the scarcity of salt and flour, the monotonous diet. Pumpkin fresh and pumpkin dried, pumpkin, pumpkin! But there was occasional merriment, too. At Mansfield the men could scarcely contain their laughter as they answered evening roll-call with additional fictitious names, pretending they were of great number, in case the Indians were listening. And with what jollity they greeted news of the *Battle of the Cowpens*, as it came to be called, when the American militia, encamped on their way to Fort Meigs, on a rainy night made a tremendous assault on the foe, which turned out to be a herd of cattle roaming in the woods!

Johnny remembered how bravely the blockhouse men would sometimes sing *Step forth, ye sons of Freedom*, and for the benefit of the girls in the loft above them, *There's nothing like the Yankee girls. The Yankee girls for me.* The stories that were told to lighten the hours; of life in the old homelands, of the hard pioneering westward, and of hunting! Johnny, too, dipped into the marvel of his story bag when he came, and he read from his Bible and from his Swedenborg volume of *Heaven and Hell*. He brought to the women and children flowers from the woods, nuts and berries, and wild herbs for brewing teas and medicines, walnut hulls and oak bark for dyeing cloth. With shy interest Johnny had gazed upon Eliza Wolf, the pretty schoolmarm at Mansfield, teaching the pale, imprisoned children their *a, b, c's* with the aid of alphabet paddles. *How strange is life,* thought lonely Johnny, *when for the love of a girl—the cold Eliza—a certain village tailor could lose his wits, and by criminy, had done it, and likely would never again be right in his head.*

Johnny had seen the women, white with anxiety, when their men went out to sow and to harvest, with sometimes a few soldiers to guard them. But at last the war was over. A treaty was made and signed by President Madison, but first by the bewildered Indian chiefs—Kilbuck, White Eyes, Captain Pipe and others, signing their doom. Parcels of former Indian lands were given them as reservations. The white people had flocked out of the blockhouses like birds from cages. The fun and frolic they had then enjoyed, log-rollings and cabin-raisings, corn-huskings, and the madcap dancing of the *scamperdown* or the *western swing.* Strangers came a-pioneering by the thousands, as eagerly as if the West were paradise itself. The frontier was pushed to the far Mississippi. Johnny Appleseed himself entered new territory, planted new orchards.

But for all his solitary grubbing and fencing, his transplanting and pruning, for all his lone, swift walking and carrying hither and yon, he could not possibly supply the settlers' demand for apple trees. "Lord, I humbly ask Thee, have I earned my heavenly reward? Still short of forty-three I am, still as hardy as a pine knot. Let me live, Lord. Let me plant for the new pioneers along the Auglaize, the St. Mary's and the Maumee. If it be Thy will, let me go into the wild lands of Indiana and Michigan and Illinois, for they seem to beckon me. Forgive me, Lord, but I've been hoarding a precious hankering to see the Mississippi before I die. Lord, I'm too poor a creature to aspire to wrasslin' with Thine angel here in the backwoods, but if only I could live to walk into Baltimore some day, wearing a good coat and shoes, and maybe a stovepipe hat, then I'd see the New-church temple raised up in Thy name." Stovepipe hat? There must have been tender mirth in heaven when that part of Johnny's prayer came winging in!

But while he was at it, there was something else he'd like to mention. Except for the convenience of growing trees on his own acreage, he cared little for personal possessions. The buckeye in his pocket to charm away the rheumatism, the meal for his mush, the fruits of the forest, the scant covering for his body, a bit of money to keep him from beggary—these were the only material necessities. But it would give him sweet pleasure to leave a piece of fertile land to his dear half sister Persis, now married, and to Nathanael and Eliza Rudd, the children of his own beloved sister Elizabeth, back east. "Lord, is that too much to ask?"

But in the moments before the stupor overtook him, Johnny heard no sure answer. And at last the Indians found him, scarcely breathing. They told afterward how he lay surrounded by an amazing medley of footprints, those of every wild creature of cave and wood. Yet Johnny bore no mark of tooth or claw. The Indians said it was because of the Book he carried in his bosom. He had often declared that it protected him from harm. They took him up gently, and carried him to their hunting camp. For in spite of treaties and reservations, they still believed it their immemorial right to hunt where their tribes had always hunted, to fish in the same streams, to make sugar in the groves which once had been theirs, and theirs only.

To this hunting ground the Indians had brought some of their squaws to do the work of the camp. There were a few children. One of them, a boy named Little Jumper, found endless delight in the monotonous beating of a small water drum. Johnny Appleseed did not consciously hear it, but in his clouded dreams it became the beat of his own footsteps, twenty years of tramping from his home country to the West, and through its wild terrain—how many steps, how many miles? In the oblivion of his illness Johnny did not feel the squaw's fingers binding the fragrant pennyroyal upon his brow, nor taste the bitter brew she forced between his lips. The odors of the cooking and the tobacco-smoking meant nothing to him, nor the barking of dogs and the jargon of talk when the day's hunting was over. The silence of the night was no deeper than the companionless silence which lay within him. By day he did not see the wild, magnificent beauty of this place, the waterfall plunging in a welter of white foam over the brink of a high ledge, over a tumble of great boulders, and around it, guarding cliff and cascade, a dark wall of hemlocks.

There came an hour when the Indian woman saw Johnny stir, and heard him, in his mounting delirium, begin to talk. The other squaws drew near, but in their ignorance they could not make out what Johnny said, although his words were compellingly spoken. The women muttered together that perhaps Johnny might be communing with the spirits. Or perhaps his bag of apple seeds was making strange medicine for him. The bag was a mysterious thing, not in itself, but because Johnny made such extraordinary use of it, ever carrying it about with him, and dipping into it inexhaustibly to sow for others. An amazing way for one to behave, for the squaws knew that it is the habit of man, whether paleface or redskin, to take, rather than to give.

"I hear the feet tramping, the feet of a missionary appleplanter," cried Johnny, out of his fever. "The feet of the pioneers—I hear them walking westward. Let me go before them—let me go. Here is fine, open ground for apple trees, here by the river of life. Comfort the pioneers. Comfort them with apples—the *Fallawater*, the *Sweet Bough*, the *Willow Twig*, the *Fall—a—water*—" Johnny's voice trailed off, as he seemed to listen. He moaned and turned his head, calling for water.

When his Indian nurse had moistened his lips, he began again. "The moon is a *Golden Pippin*. The sun is a *Red Astrachan*. The earth—what is Earth?" he demanded of the squaw. She shook her head and drew back, shivering, for she was afraid of Johnny's strangeness, and his fevered babble. "Earth?" inquired Johnny of the timorous squaw, and his parched lips tried to smile. "Why, don't you know that Earth is an apple?" he cried triumphantly. "The master said so. He held Earth up and turned it in his hand. 'Earth is a round apple,' the master said."

Then Johnny sank into a restless sleep. And he dreamed that he stood at the gates of the New Jerusalem, which were like the doors of a great temple. A child was there, beating a drum. Johnny tried talking with the child, first in the Indian tongue, then in English. But the boy only looked at him out of his beady black eyes and went on pounding the drum. From within the gates could be heard the rushing of wings, so vast that it sounded like the sweep of falling water. Johnny wanted to enter, but it seemed he couldn't as long as the Indian boy stood there. He had a dreadful feeling of failure and disappointment, and with that his dream fell into confusion, until at last it faded away into sleep, deep and healing.

After a long time, Johnny woke up. The fever was gone, and in its stead a blessed quietness and peace. He did not know where he was, but the question did not disturb him. He saw the hemlocks standing tall and dark above him. He saw the white water flashing over the cliff, and heard its rushing music. A copper-skinned boy pounded on a water drum. The face of an Indian woman, dark and kind, bent over Johnny. "Been long time sick," she said. "Johnny heap sick. Johnny drink, now. Johnny get well." She slipped her broad hand under his head, while he drank the brew she offered.

He remembered, then, how God had struck him down in the forest. Foolish Johnny, foolish mortal, to get so riled up over the damage done by the frost! The trees themselves were not injured. There would be another summer, warm and kind as the hands of an Indian woman. There would be the rose-cupped blossoms, the fruit flushed with ripening. Praise God, Johnny Appleseed would carry on his work for the pioneers. In Michigan and Indiana the boughs of his trees would yet hang thick with shining apples—the *Fallawater*, the *Sweet Bough*, the *Willow Twig*.

And *good la*, wouldn't humble Johnny have been dumfounded if he had known that his name had appeared in print, and in faraway England! Only last January the Manchester Swedenborgians had published a brief account of Johnny's work. *There is in the western country a very extraordinary missionary of the New Jerusalem. A man has appeared who seems to be almost independent of corporal wants and sufferings. He goes barefooted, can sleep anywhere, in house or out ... and lives upon the coarsest and most scanty fare ... He procures what books he can of the New Church, travels to the remote settlements and leaves them wherever he can find readers. ... This man for years past has been in the employment of bringing into cultivation in numberless places in the wilderness small patches ... of ground, and then sowing apple seeds and rearing nurseries. These become valuable as the settlements approximate, and the profits* (enable) *him to print the writings of Emanuel Swedenborg and distribute them through the western settlements of the United States.*

As soon as Johnny was able, he made his slow and feeble return to the settlements. He was a sight to behold. To lighten his burdens, he wore his cooking pot on his head. His shirt was nothing more than a burlap bag, with holes cut for neck and arms. ... "Pa, Ma, here's Uncle Johnny Appleseed again!" The children's cries were joyous. And the woman, mothering him: "Lawk-a-mercy me, Johnny! Now you just take that rusty kittle off your head and set down and rest your poor pindlin' self. Here's milk and honey, and fresh board-cake. I'll have you fattened up in no time if you'll stay, and I'll cut you out a new tow shirt. I declare, it's enough to break a body's heart to lay eyes on you!" ... And the man, squeezing a chuckle past the lump in his throat: "Johnny, you cussed ol' wander-foot, you had us plenty worried! Now you jus' plan to bide with us a spell. 'Twill rightly jubilate us, having you around."

1822

WILLOW TWIG

To REACH Johnny's camp we go about fourteen miles as the crow flies," remarked young Bartley. "Haven't noticed we're crows," objected Matthew. "Eighteen miles as the woodchuck goes, I'd say." The boys laughed, rejoicing in Matthew's wit. Laughter came so easy this fair morning. Youth, adventure ahead, the fresh and beautiful world—surely yonder redbud was never of earth, but a rosy cloud set adrift from dawn and snared by the branches. Surely the wood-nymphs themselves had hung against the new green curtains of their house the carved white ornaments which mortal man called *dogwood*. Swift flight, saucy flirt, rapturous melody—the birds were everywhere. And five happy, teen-aged boys were setting forth from their various homes in

Richland County for Johnny Appleseed's nursery on the headwaters of the Sandusky River. The rough way they took, once deer path, Indian trail, army road, now carried travelers from Mansfield to Bucyrus, a settlement only this year being surveyed. Between the two lived perhaps five or six families. Mansfield, while a trading center with three stores and two taverns, was still "backwoods." Galion was yet but a maple grove.

This morning's travelers were Joseph Welch and Matthew Curran, Jonathan Beach and Richard Corydon. They were going as company for young Bartley, whose father was sending him for saplings. Last, but certainly the largest of the troop, was Pardner, Bartley's horse, which would bear the young trees homeward tomorrow. At present he carried Joe Welch and Dick Corydon. Each of the boys had a gun, a blanket, and a bag of provisions. Their chatter jumped from subject to subject. Girls, for instance.

"Hear that Effie Hamlin and Sedelia Brothers hung a wishbone above Hamlin's door, and were waiting and snickering when in you walked, Senator Bartley," Joe teased. "The first to walk under the wishbone—it's a sure sign. Reckon you'll live to marry Effie."

"I could go farther and fare worser," answered Bartley, unabashed. He was so full of the boldness and spirit of his ambition to become a statesman like his father, Mordecai, that his chums had nicknamed him *Senator*. "For that matter, Joe Welch," he now gave back, "half an eye can see you're kind of sweet on Sedelia."

Joe grinned. He would be as bold as Senator. "Sedelia's got the rosiest cheeks in all the West," he drawled, and winked at Matt.

"Shucks!" exclaimed Dick Corydon, so young as to be completely disgusted with this kind of talk. "Are we sitting 'round the hearth with our knittin', or are we goin' man-size through the woods and marshes to Johnny Appleseed's?"

"We're goin', Bud, man-size we're goin'." Joe flipped the fox tail dangling from Dick's cap. Without warning a song rolled from his throat, like notes from an English hunting horn:

> Our sweethearts, wives and children
> Will meet us with three cheers,
> Crying huzza, huzza, huzza,
> There's the gallant volunteers,
> There's the boys of Ohio!

"You began in the middle," quibbled Dick, although he loved Joe's rousing *huzzas*. "Besides, it's an ol' way-back-yonder song." Being so fond of one another he and Joe reveled in exchanging banter.

"What of it, Bud?" Joe gave the fox tail another tweak. "Couldn't expect a trundle-bed boy like you to have any senterment for a tune that was sung in the blockhouse when I was a kid in skirts and the Injuns besieging us." Suddenly, with easy strength, Joe lifted Dick from the saddle and dropped him neatly to earth. "Babe that you are, you're too big for this horse," he roared, "and riding past your turn. Me, too." He swung himself down. "Up with you, Matt, and you, Jonathan. The Senator can walk a while longer, since we're favorin' him with our company."

"S'pose you're sure Johnny has any saplings left," Jonathan Beach speculated, when the laughter had subsided. " 'Most all the new orchards in Springfield township's been started from that one nursery."

"Johnny told Father to send for the trees about this time," answered Senator. "He said he'd be waiting. Johnny never breaks a promise."

"When the nursery's emptied of trees, guess he will go on somewhere else."

"West," said Senator. "Johnny works a little farther west each year."

"What if he gets so far west he can't get back?" asked Dick.

"Never you fret. There's that sister at Mansfield Johnny's so fond of, Mistress Persis Broom, and her four daughters. Besides, as long as ol' Johnny has any young, unsold trees in these parts, or friends, either, he will be coming back." Senator spoke with certainty. "That fel-

low gets over the ground. He will be going and coming
'til he drops in his tracks."

"Must be pretty old by now," mused young Dick.

"In all the times Johnny's stayed at our place," answered Senator, "he's never said. But he's so brown and
wrinkled 'gainst the weather, we've been calling him 'old'
for years."

"Bet we call him '*old* Johnny' 'cause we like him," observed Jonathan, "same as you call your dog you think a
sight of, '*old* Trip,' when maybe Trip's just a pup."

"Heard a new story about Johnny the other day."
Matt's voice was loud above the sudden drumming of a
partridge in the woods. "Seems that Johnny bought six
stoneware plates in Mansfield. 'Now what on earth d'you
want with all those dishes?' someone asked. But you know
ol' Johnny can joke a-plenty when he wants to shy away
from the real answer. So he up and answered, 'Why, man,
by having six plates I shan't need to wash 'em but once
a week!' But it turned out that he went straight as he could
walk and gave the plates to a poor family. That's Johnny
Appleseed for you."

"Elias Slocum, over at Ashland, was telling Father how
one winter he gave Johnny a pair of good, sound boots,"
said Senator. "But next time Johnny came in sight, his feet
were as bare as the day he was born. 'Johnny,' asked Elias,
looking him straight in the eye, 'did I, or did I not, give
you a pair of good boots?' 'You did, Elias, and God bless

you for it,' answered Johnny, 'for I met a poor traveler bound for the West, with never a shoe to his feet, and snow on the ground.' So that was that," Senator concluded.

But after a moment he went on, for he treasured a hoard of stories about Johnny. "My mother offered to make Johnny a warm linsey-woolsey coat. The women roundabout worry how bare he goes. But Johnny said, 'Thank you kindly, ma'am, but I'd like it of coarse tow cloth.' He stood over Mother, and showed how he wanted it. When she'd finished, it was nothing but a long sack affair, all of a piece, that went over his head and over his nether shirt. Mother was disappointed. 'I declare, Johnny,' she said, 'you put me in mind of the one in the Bible—*there comes a poor man in vile raiment.*' 'Ma'am,' answered Johnny, soft-spoken as a wood pigeon, 'the humbler I walk the earth, the prouder I shall wear the garments of glory.' "

"Here's one," Joe offered. "Not so long ago Dave Hunter was comin' up from Green township to pay his taxes at Mansfield, when he met Johnny Appleseed. They bespoke one another, and sat on a log to talk, Dave sharing his corn cakes with Johnny. 'Twasn't long before Johnny was urging Dave not to put off getting himself an orchard. 'Why, man alive!' cried Dave, kinda provoked, 'I've got eight orphaned brothers and sisters to do for. Me, with the almighty luxury of a fruit orchard?' 'Yes, you!' retorted Johnny, with a grin. 'I can supply you with sixty young trees. The pay doesn't matter, compared to the need of your orphans for apples. Now lad, you call on my brother-in-law, William Broom, who's growing my trees on his farm. Tell him I sent you.' And by cracky," cried Joe, "Dave got his trees! He's layin' out to become a fruit grower on a big scale, all on account of Johnny Appleseed."

"They say the orchard Johnny planted on the Carter-Springer farm near Ashland is the biggest he's ever planted in Ohio—thirty acres," said Jonathan. "Johnny knew Springer a long time back, in Pittsburgh. Guess he knows 'most everybody in the state."

"Johnny will never eat at table. Says he's too poor a body," Matt contributed, chuckling. "He will never sleep in a bed. Fears it would make a softy out of 'im. Seems he makes himself as ornery uncomfortable as he can. That reminds me," continued Matt, "once Johnny slept the night on the barroom floor of Slocum's tavern. Soon as he left next morning, Elias found a five-dollar note, and hurried after Johnny. 'You must've dropped this," he said. Johnny searched his pockets. 'Yes, it's mine, Elias,' he answered, and in no hurry whatever to take the money, 'but you shouldn't have gone to all the trouble of returning it to me.' Did you ever?" cried Matt, with fresh astonishment.

And so, with Johnny Appleseed's nursery their goal, the boys discussed the man himself. They talked of him as one familiar and beloved, and they talked of him as an oddity and a mystery. Unknowingly, their talk fostered and enlarged his legend, for they spoke in wonder and fond amusement, and with a little exaggeration that would grow as the years gathered their luster about him.

"Bet Johnny will yarn us some yarns tonight," declared Dick.

"It's like as if, along with his seed sack, Johnny carries a bag stuffed chock-full of stories," mused Jonathan. From above his head a cardinal seemed to be cheering those words.

A bag of stories. What whimsy! But Joe Welch, blushing, covered his embarrassment at Jonathan's romanticizing by raising his gun. "Watch me hit that little squidgicum of a worm on yon twig," he blustered. Against the sun the boys saw the caterpillar in tiny creeping silhouette. *Bang,* and the caterpillar was no more! Delight in Joe's marksmanship shone on every countenance.

"Father said we weren't to carry any game into Johnny's camp," Senator warned, not meaning to be funny. But Joe turned to Dick. "Young 'un, go skin the worm an' hang him out o' reach of the bears. We'll pick up his precious carcass on the way back, and have us a feast." Oh, Joe was a card! There followed a mile's length of laughter and boisterous jokes. The boys sobered, unafraid but wary, when they spied a file of mounted Indians approaching.

"On their way from the reservations to trade at Mansfield," muttered Senator, "with their deer hams and maple sugar."

"How! How! You go—?" The Indians pulled up, their spokesman grunting the salutation and question.

"How! We go—" Out of mischief Joe withheld the information as to his party's destination.

The eyes of the spokesman glittered from out the leathery mask of his face. He and his companions rode on, glumly. But presently he came galloping back. He leaned low from his saddle. His lips drew back in a horrid grimace. "Injuns know boys go Johnny Appleseed lodge," he hissed. "Injuns know Johnny wait at place of willows." He wheeled and cantered off to join his fellows. The boys heard them whooping with triumphant laughter.

"Once you could shoot 'em, and no questions asked," Joe grumbled. "But now you'd be hauled into court. Times've changed," he added, mournfully.

Speaking of the "times" sent the boys into talk of the growing country; the carving out of new Ohio counties; the admission to statehood of Indiana and Illinois. Feeling progressively modern, these young citizens spoke of the exciting brand-new plans for building a canal the length of Ohio, perhaps several canals. And *by jingo*, if you could stand long enough on the banks of the Ohio River, 'twas said you could make out the names of forty different steamboats plying up, or down! And what farthest backwoodsman had not heard of *Walk-in-the-Water*, the steamer on Lake Erie!

"Wonder if I'll ever live long enough to have me a ride on a steamboat," reflected Dick, doubtfully.

"Could be more'n dreamery, Bud," Joe assured him.

"But it's likely none of us will live to see the National Pike laid across Ohio," declared Matt. "Pa says everybody is growling over the way the pike's eating up the dollars, and it no farther than over the hill at Wheeling."

At noon the boys stopped to eat at Palmer Springs, source of Spring Run and the Sandusky. After skirting a camp of Delawares, they reached Johnny's nursery, lying between the run and a ridge of knolls. Within a few years Leesville would stand here. Some day a state highway would follow the Warrior's Road which ran north past Johnny's nursery. He had a canny intelligence for planting where pioneers would surely build their towns, and did indeed—strategic places to which trail and stream transported men and goods.

The boys saw thickets of willows growing along the banks of the run. They saw the living willow-brush fence with which Johnny had enclosed his nursery. Now, in the Spring, the fence sprouted heads of leafy twigs. Johnny and two other men were digging up young apple trees. Johnny dropped his implement, his face alight with pleasure when he saw the boys. He came forward, his feet caked with damp earth. "So you've come, young friends," he said. "This is George Wood and David Gill, from down Whetstone Creek. You see I'm about to clear out this nursery."

The Whetstone men soon had their trees bundled and carried to their pirogue, which rocked gently on the stream among the willows. When they had gone, Johnny said the boys must rest from their travel, and he from his labor. All drank deeply from the nearby spring. Johnny took a bit of snuff, a pulverized mixture of swamp willow bark and tobacco he had got from the Indians. It made him a little sleepy. He stretched himself out on a broad log, for like his friends the woods-creatures, he followed the simple rule of resting when he was tired. The boys, quiet for his sake, saw him dozing there—the famous Johnny Appleseed—spare and sinewy, his flesh deeply scarred and weathered, his hair flowing, his garb scant and shabby. In the east, and in the flourishing towns along the Ohio, gentlemen were wearing their striped nankeens and their velvet-collared claw hammers, but never in his life did Johnny Appleseed hide his simple self behind a high cravat or satin waistcoat. Rich manor house and assembly chamber might have their fluted columns and delicate moldings, their marble chimney pieces and elegant ornament, but here, in this green willow-fringed glade was Johnny Appleseed's little campfire, his log couch, his rude shelter of elm bark.

Resting time over, the work of taking up Mordecai's

trees was soon done, for when Johnny moved, he moved quickly. He explained his methods. "Say that I sow my seeds on unclaimed land, like here," he began. "A planter with but two hands, an ax, and a pointed stick will choose open ground having no big trees to cut down, and along streams and trails, so the saplings can be carried out. I clear out the underbrush and sow the seeds. I put up some sort of fence. Next year the seedlings are standing thick-set as yonder spring beauties. I weed, and give the sturdier trees a chance to grow and spread out. Sometimes I like to plant in a natural opening in the woods. A poke of the finger into the deep, loose mold, and the seed is sown. Blossoms for the wild bees: some day an apple for the traveler; an apple for the deer. Of course I prune my nurseries from time to time. Takes tendin', takes traipsin'.

"When I plant on a man's farm, it's agreed that half the trees shall be his own orchard. When anyone wants my trees, I set down an order in writing for the landowner to let Captain *So-and-So* have a certain number. Cap'n pays me if he's able. If his pocket be empty, he trades something, or he gets the trees for nothing, and God go with 'em. That reminds me, d'you lads know Martin Mason, over near Perrysville? I planted for him eight years ago, and sold off my own share, part of them to Captain Eben Rice." A smile made crisscrosses of Johnny's wrinkles. "Bless my soul if Cap'n's granddaughter, little Rosella, hasn't given the name of 'Johnnyweed' to the fennel I planted thick around the Rice home! Some folks might not take that as a compliment, fennel being so rank-smelling. But I hold it an honor. Wish I could plant the fennel in every Ohio county! Brew a tea from it, and you've got a sure cure for the ague!" The boys couldn't laugh, not with Johnny's face so bright with his faith in the dog fennel. *That vile pest of field and roadside—oh, planter, because you are Johnny Appleseed of the giving heart and hands—shall we not smile, and forgive you?*

"Now, boys," Johnny went on, "we'll bundle and tie these saplings with willow withes and wrap them with wet moss for packing them home. Then we'll have supper."

David Gill and George Wood had brought Johnny a gift of potatoes, now roasting in hot ashes. Johnny tested them. "In two shakes, or three, they'll be ready," he advised. After he and the boys had washed themselves, and while they waited on the potatoes, Johnny sat cross-legged on his log. The robins were calling from the willows, loud and imperious. Johnny put his fingers to his lips and imitated them, so like that the boys were astonished. They sat in a kind of frozen joy as Johnny chittered like a squirrel, bleated like a doe, barked like a fox. In turn he hooted like an owl, squawked like a heron, or uttered the sweet notes of gentler birds. There were answers, far and faint. Nearer, coming nearer, were timid rustlings, hesitant small patterings, soft whir of wings. From leafy coverts of bough and thicket bright eyes gleamed, bright plumage shone. The furred and the feathered—they were all around, lured by Johnny Appleseed. The moment was enchantment, tense, spellbinding, frail as a bubble. Johnny and the boys, the glade with its wild flowers and creatures, the swaying willow fronds and glinting water, the iridescent spring light—all were held within that expanding moment, while its walls trembled in fragile transience.

"Ah, the dear wildlings!" Johnny's sigh was scarcely audible. The motion of sliding to his feet was quiet. Yet the bubble burst. *Scamper, rush,* and there was only stodgy old Pardner, hobbled, reaching greedily for young leaves. The potatoes were drawn out, hot and gritty. Johnny offered them, with salt from his housekeeping store. The boys spread out their bread and venison. Tin cup in hand, each gulped down sassafras tea from Johnny's bubbling pot.

Young Dick, knowing that Johnny abhorred meat, felt impelled to ask if he did not sometimes go hungry. "The Lord spreads my table from the first wild strawberry to the last papaw and persimmon," answered Johnny. "From the Indians I've learned what roots to cook. In exchange for wild fruits, or apple seeds, or for my help in husking corn and chopping wood, the settlers give me milk and honey and meal."

Supper over, Johnny seemed in mood for entertainment. These fresh-faced boys visiting his lonely camp—

how pleasant to have them! The fire replenished to leaping brightness, Johnny showed the boys an Indian contest
of strength and endurance, a tug of war between two,
with fingers interlocked. It was exciting and painful.
Johnny's fingers were as hard as steel. Next, he invited
them to join in psalm-singing. They sang ballads from
the Isles, tales of derring-do, and long laments of love. In
a high nasal quaver Johnny soloed an original composi-
tion of Adam Swinehart's, one of his pioneer friends in
Carroll County. Eleven verses recounted the hanging of
Major André, the captured spy, in 1780:

> Come, all you bold Americans,
>   I pray you now draw near,
> I'll sing you a small ditty,
>   your spirits for to cheer,
> Concerning a young gentleman,
>   whose age was twenty-two;
> He fought for North America;
>   his heart was just and true.

> .   .   .   .   .

> When Andrew was executed,
>   he was both meek and mild;
> He looked on his spectators,
>   and pleasantly he smiled,
> Which caused our generals to fall back
>   and made their hearts to bleed;
> They wished poor Major Andrew clear,
>   and Arnold in his stead.

To annul the effects of this tragic tale, Johnny and his guests sang ancient rounds, and they played singing games, hilariously cavorting around the fire. When they were spent with laughter, and resting, Dick Corydon asked Johnny for stories. "Speaking of apples," began Johnny, "Martin Mason was but one of many who's had my order for trees. I planted for Martin his first spring in Ashland County. The next winter was keen cold. For forty days snow lay deep, and deeper. Martin had about as many children as he had freckles. So did Jacob, his brother. Took a mountain o' bread to feed them all. That cold time the Masons run out of meal. Their only cow had died from browsing on buckeye buds. No milk or butter, no meat or potatoes. Martin and Jake went by ox-drawn sled to Stibb's mills, near Wooster, but when they got there the mill wasn't grinding, 'count of the ice.

"The miller let the brothers have a few bushels of whole corn. Going home they met an Indian, and inquired about game. Indian said he'd just treed a 'coon, which they could have for the getting. So, in the bitter cold, the Masons cut down the giant tree and captured the animal. At home again, there was feasting on 'coon meat and hominy. A few days later came the Indians Billy Mature and Jim Jerk with a bear they'd killed. Eight dollars in silver Martin paid them, and glad to. The bear meat tided them over 'til the weather bettered and the mill was running. God preserved the Masons. God sent the Indians," declared Johnny.

From beyond the ridge an owl hooted. In the wilderness dark the sound seemed significant. Joe started up, gun in hand. Senator reached for his own weapon, for these boys had been nurtured on tales of Indian trickery that led to attack.

"Pshaw!" scolded Johnny. "It's but an owl. The Indians—they're sly as animals, and mischievous—how they love to whoop and yell and scowl and grunt, just to scare the white women when their men are away! But since the war they're harmless, save when they've drunk too much 'Sandusky water.' They're like children." Johnny smiled. "When first I came to Ohio there was a cousin of mine had a cabin not far from Old Town, a Miami village above Byesville, in Guernsey County. Cousin John had a baby girl, a little creature with curls as bright as if the sun never left her. One day she vanished from her play in the clearing. John grabbed his gun and rushed off to Old Town. He believed the Indians had taken her in revenge, for he'd once killed a fellow named Hole-in-the-Ear he'd caught stealing a dressed deer. But Old Town claimed to know nothing of the lost child. So John returned home and bade his grieving wife farewell. He'd go two hundred miles to another Miami Village. Anger against the savages and anxiety for the child lent speed to his going. On the third evening he came upon a night's encampment, and found his beloved babe, unharmed. 'Injuns no steal papoose,' declared the red men. 'Injuns borrow. Show squaw white child. Squaw never see hair like shine of sun.'

"And crafty—oh my!" Johnny laughed. "My friend Abraham Baughman once bought from an Indian a scrawny calf. The next spring this fellow came to Baughman's, and saw the calf fine and healthy. 'Calf growed much. Want more money,' he demanded. For the sake of peace, Abraham paid. And tuck me under, boys," said Johnny, "if the next spring the same thing didn't happen! Well, Abraham knew there would be another spring, in fact, several. So he fatted the calf and killed it for meat.

"Oh, yes, I know the Indians well," declared Johnny. "I knew most of their old villages, Coshocton and Cranetown, Old Chillicothe and Lower Shawneetown, a whole string of 'em. I've known their chiefs, Blue Jacket and Tarhe the Crane, Leatherlips, Seneca John. The Indians have taught me many things, and shared with me their food. Lads, have no fear of the owl. Now let us sleep. It is time." Johnny curled himself up on his log. The boys, conscious of the vast dark beyond the fire, felt suddenly deserted. "I've heard this is snake country," faltered Dick, casting a suspicious look at his bed of boughs.

"So it is," answered Johnny, cheerfully. "They come from the great marshes roundabout. In the night they may seek the warmth of the boughs beneath you. But lie still, and they will do you no harm. Once, God forgive me, in sudden fear I killed a rattler reared to strike. It has troubled me ever since." Johnny lifted his head and saw the eyes of the boys wide and solemn in the firelight. "Now tut, tut, lads," he chided, gently. "The noises you may hear are those of the woods-creatures going about their business. Look at the stars above you. Look long enough, and you will see God's bright host. *He shall give his angels charge over thee.* It's promised," said Johnny.

Balm of faith! The night was a tall mansion, curtained with sleep, with silence.

The boys never forgot their stay at that "place of willows." Jonathan Beach, the imaginative one, remembered Johnny Appleseed as the mystic who could see angels among the stars, who could call out the little hiders of the woods. Young Bartley remembered him as the pioneer, human and real, mingling with, and loved by the settlers. And he remembered him, playing and singing with five lively boys in a firelit glade. Years later, when Bartley had actually become a senator, he wrote of Johnny in the Mansfield *Shield and Banner:*

> He had full many a story to tell,
> And goodly hymns that he sung right well:
> He tossed up the babies, and joined the boys
> In many a game full of fun and noise.
>
> And he seemed so hearty, in work or play,
> Men, women and boys all urged him to stay.

The senator went on to say, more notably:

...his memory will linger in the hearts of...generations
...to come, and their children will learn to revere the
decaying monuments [the apple trees] *of his industry and*
benevolence as the memorials of one whose character,
though unbalanced, swayed to the brighter side of human
nature.

1838

SWEET BOUGH

SALLY BEECHER was fourteen that April when *Chapman's Floating Theatre* swung around the great bend of the Ohio River and tied up below the Indiana town of Mount Vernon. As in preceding years, the Negro orchestra of three marched up the bluff and into the public square. Their respective blowing, tootling, and pounding of key bugle, fife and drum was so spirited as to make the most critical forget that their gold braid was somewhat tarnished.

But Wilbur Chapman, who followed, was elegant from head to toe in silk hat, bottle-green coat tightly buttoned, fawn-colored pantaloons, lemon-yellow gloves, and an *air!* It was an air becoming to the owner of a floating theater. It suited this veteran English-born actor who had performed on the London stage, who could, if necessary, fill any rôle from that of "heavy man" to "low comedian," and whose troupe of accomplished sons and daughters had made his boat famous along the rivers of the West.

In Mr. Chapman's wake this morning was his youngest son, Harry, who had a dog on a leash. The printed dodgers scattered in Mount Vernon a week ago by Chapman's advance man had proclaimed the dog as "Penny, the pertest little pantomimist on the American stage today."

His English-born speech punctuated with broad *a's* and neglected *r's*, Mr. Chapman addressed the assembled Mount Vernonites. They listened with delight to the magnificent adjectives describing the entertainment which the *Floating Theatre* was offering this season; and the heart of every villager, young and old, swelled with self-esteem as the actor poured out a honeyed stream of compliments.

"The Chapman family is always greatly exhilarated upon arriving at Mount Vernon, to receive the bounty of her unfailing hospitality and generous patronage," declared Wilbur Chapman. "And not least, to renew pleasant friendship with the finest and most intelligent of river folk. We have been coming here since our flatboat days, when all we had was an auditorium on a barge. But now, below yon bluff, behold a magnificent steamer, carrying a real theater, and properly navigated by a skilled pilot and engineer. There are other floating theaters on the western waters, but none on whose stage the members of one family perform with such remarkable ability, such art. I would not make so bold and unblushing a declaration, my friends, had not the acting profession itself paid us the compliment." Mr. Chapman went on at some length, breadth, and thickness, and then he paused to sniff, delicately. "As we came downstream," he said, "the most heavenly fragrance drifted out to us from your shores. 'Ah-h!' thought I, 'the orchards of Mount Vernon are in bloom!' These sweet blossoming boughs, my good friends, do they not breathe eloquently of the very soul of Mount Vernon, queen village of the river? Are they not redolent of the trust which flowers between us?" Another sniff, more prolonged, more blissful. "Ah-h-h, never so halcyon a time for the Chapmans to arrive at Mount Vernon than the lovely apple blossom time!"

Mr. Chapman now shook hands all around. Penny went through a few of his tricks to the tempo of the fife; drum and bugle accenting the fun with sudden thumps and blares, and the villagers full of merriment because of him.

Sally Beecher, on her way home from *North & McFadden's* with a spool of silk for Grandma, heard and saw everything. As always, her heart was filled with longing to attend a performance in a floating theater. Except for Grandma, who thought that theater-going led straight to "the bad place," Sally felt certain that she was the only person on the entire river's length never to push her fifty cents through the ticket window of a theater-boat.

Across the Square, Sally spied her Uncle Joe, who was a bachelor and had a farm and apple orchard two miles up-river. She slipped around to whisper in his ear. "Wish Granny would let me go. Just once!" she added, tragically.

Uncle Joe patted her hand. "I've told 'er over and over 'twouldn't hurt you a mite," he said. "Blamed if I don't plan to come to town every night while the boat is docked." He grinned. "And blamed if I don't bring Chapman an armful of apple boughs. Notion jus' struck me, him speaking so pretty of 'em."

"Stop in on your way tonight, Uncle Joe," begged Sally. "Maybe Grandma would give in when she sees the flowers. Sin and apple blossoms don't go together, do they?" A sob rose suddenly in her throat. She turned away, quickly, longing to run. But Granny said that a fourteen-year-old girl should walk the streets of Mount Vernon like a lady. So there was time for her to calm down before reaching home. At once Grandma spoke up. "I heard the goings-on in the Square. S'pose you saw it."

"Yes," answered Sally. "I saw Uncle Joe, too. He promised to stop in tonight on his way to—"

"To the place of lost souls on that boat," finished Grandma, grimly.

But within Sally's young heart hope had never died. She was a dutiful girl, but today she was highly industrious. She cleaned out the fireside cupboards of her own free will. She prepared most of the noon meal. She made eight quilt blocks, employing her tiniest and straightest stitches. Grandma praised her.

At first, when Uncle Joe appeared at their door that evening, they could see little of him, for he was quite concealed by the great armful of blossoming apple boughs which he carried. All of April seemed to drift into Granny's kitchen on their fragrance. "There's nothing in the world so almighty sweet," she crooned, rising to sniff at the lavish bouquet.

"You mean me?" joked Uncle Joe. "Or do you mean Johnny?" He glanced backward as a figure stepped out of the dusk.

"Uncle Johnny Appleseed!" cried Sally, and Grandma held up her hands in astonishment. "Johnny! Where on earth did you come from?"

"Been planting along the Wabash," answered Johnny, smiling. "Being so near, thought I'd come over and see how Joe's orchard was doing."

"Aunt Sarah," demanded Uncle Joe, without the least delay, "why don't you leave Sally go to the entertainment? Johnny's going."

"Johnny Appleseed!" cried Granny, staring and open-mouthed. "You mean to stand there and say you're going to—to—" Grandma choked.

"Yes, ma'am," answered Johnny, mildly. "Joe here tells me the folks that run the boat are named Chapman. So I'm right cur'us to see them. They might be kin of mine. Reckon you know, ma'am, that Chapman's the name I was born with—John Chapman."

Grandma sank down on the lid of the dye-tub, as the nearest support. She chewed her fingernails, deep in thought. "Sally Beecher!" she cried. "Bring me my reticule and my shawl and bonnet. Get your own wrappings. The Lord forgive me if I do wrong, but I've got to see Johnny Appleseed in a theater. Besides, he will keep us from evil."

"No, ma'am. With your help God will do that," answered Johnny.

How Sally's feet flew to bring the wraps! How she trembled as she walked silently with the others to the bluff and down to the boat under the light of burning flares!

The theater was already darkened. The play had begun. Beyond rows of strange and mysterious silhouettes of other villagers, beyond the flickering footlights, the actors walked on and off in make-believe, yet with such reality that the people trembled and sighed, laughed and wept. "Ah, can't you see how this lovely flirt is breaking my heart?" cried the hero of the "Melo-drama," turning to the audience in tragic plea.

"Yes, but make 'er give in. You can do it," advised an old farmer from the front row. It was as real as that!

Following the play one of the Chapman sons performed as a juggler. The dog Penny did his amazing little tricks. The next act brought on stage a lanky man in a long black coat. He stalked out with a Bible under one arm and demanded to know what in holy heaven's name had become of "that there mourners' bench." Two scared devils in red underwear and black tails scampered in with the bench and scuttled off stage. A half-dozen men and women filed in, mournfully. Sunbonnets, blue jeans, muddy boots— they were backwoods folk come to a religious camp meeting. Lots of shoutin', plenty of prayin', tearful mournin' over ridiculous sins. Preacher and mourners worked themselves up until they were shaking and jigging. The burlesque was about to turn into a wild song-and-dance number when a voice was heard from the audience. It was a voice both fervent and gentle. "Lord, forgive these poor show folks for taking Thy name in vain. Lord, forgive them for mocking the praise-meetings held in worship of Thee. Lord, forgive—"

Wilbur Chapman, proprietor of the *Floating Theatre*, rushed to the footlights, coat tails flying. He waved preacher and mourners away. Turning to the audience and about to speak, he fell silent. For the people seemed to have forgotten him, and all the play-acting. They were crowding around an old, gray-haired man. "It's Johnny!" they were crying. "It's dear old Johnny Appleseed!"

Sally saw Uncle Joe hastening stageward. She saw him holding up the sheaf of apple boughs. Above the talk she could not hear his words, but he was saying, "Mr. Chapman, I—I—" Uncle Joe stammered a little. "It's apple blossom time, I guess, and that's Johnny Appleseed back there. He's—"

"—a better man than I," interrupted Chapman. He relaxed, good-naturedly. "And far more popular, I see. I've heard of Johnny Appleseed, but never did I think I'd see the night when he'd break up my show."

"He didn't come for that," answered Uncle Joe. "He's a friendly fellow and when he heard your name's the same as his, he thought to meet you. *Chapman*—that's his name, too."

"You don't say!" cried the actor. He ordered the wall lights rekindled, the curtain lowered. "The entertainment was almost over, anyway," he said. "And now Wilbur and John Chapman are going to talk kinship. I'd be proud—"

Those of the villagers who remained had a treat that evening, listening to the conversation between these two men, both famous in the West, yet so completely different. No blood relationship could be traced, but it made no dif-

ference. For almost at once Johnny announced, his face
alight with that love for all men which illumined his life,
"Wilbur Chapman is my brother." Whereupon the actor
took out his handkerchief, blowing his nose and wiping
away sudden tears. "I'll tell you what, Johnny," he said,
"that camp-meeting act has always been a great laugh
maker, but never again shall it be said of the Messrs. Chapman that they present anything which may offend a good
man like you."

"Pshaw," whispered Johnny, modestly. "But I thank
you, brother Wilbur."

And what about Grandma, all this time? Flushed cheeks
and sparkling eyes made her look but half her age, what
with being so fascinated by that "Melo-drama," in which
right had triumphed mightily over wrong. Then had
come the thrill of Johnny's fearless prayer, just as she herself was ready to shout "Shame, shame!" at the top of her
voice. She said as much, now, looking sternly at Mr. Chapman. "I'd a-never stepped foot on your boat again, sir,"
she declared, regally. "But now, since you promise re-
spectable entertainment, 'twouldn't surprise me if Sally
and I don't come every night you're here. I'll see how we
sleep tonight before I say for certain."

This speech was taken seriously by all, and Sally swallowed it in such gulps as to render her speechless. Mr.
Chapman now introduced his family. There was William, who had made his theatrical début in New York ten

years ago: George, who had such a fine ballad-singing
voice as to wring the heart out of the coldest listener:
Caroline, the most accomplished of all: Harry, who was
especially gifted in farce and burletta: Therese, a fair
young thing not far from Sally's age. Harry ran to haul
up a huge catfish from the slatted cage which trailed the
steamer, for all the Chapmans were enthusiastic anglers,
and often, while waiting in make-up and fantastic costume for cues, would be watching their fishing lines.
Harry had the fish cleaned in a jiffy, and presented to
Granny with his courtliest bow. Bewitched, she extended
an invitation to Therese to call on Sally. The two young
girls smiled shyly at one another, happy at the prospect
of becoming friends.

Mr. Chapman, who never did things by halves, simply
bowled Mount Vernon over the next day when he re-
named his boat. His sons and a workman from the village
did the painting in such a short time, and in such huge letters that it was breath-taking—CHAPMAN'S APPLE
BLOSSOM THEATER!

Yes, sir! And then didn't the Ohio River countryside
pour the gifts into that steamboat—pecans gathered last
year from the nearby Wabash River bottoms: bacon from
Barter's pork-packing house: corn meal from the grist
mills: smoked venison hams: laces and ribbons! And apple blossoms—why, the theater's stage was banked with
them!

Although Johnny attended no more performances, he and Mr. Wilbur enjoyed several long and pleasant talks. The actor was so impressed with the old missionary planter as to tell the villagers he had determined to proclaim his kinship with Johnny up and down the rivers, and that he intended to give many performances in honor of "the most popular man in the West." It would not only bring good will and larger audiences to the theater boat, but a great deal of personal satisfaction to its owner. Lastly, Mr. Chapman announced that he would sell tickets at half price for the final performance at Mount Vernon, and that George would sing a beautiful new ballad composed by the Chapmans, all about Johnny Appleseed and the sweet boughs of spring. "We shall do honor to the beloved old fellow," promised the actor.

But when the great night arrived, Johnny Appleseed had slipped away, no one knew where. Then everyone realized how very unlike Johnny it would have been had he stayed to receive such laurels of praise. Any other man, perhaps—but oh, not Johnny! Somehow it touched and warmed every heart that he had gone—so humble a man as he!

1842

SEEK-NO-FURTHER*

EVAN MCNEILL crouched in the tall grass. He was playing a secret game of his own, a game of spotting a rare landmark in this Illinois prairie, where stood the lone McNeill homestead. He peeped above the nodding grass heads. A half mile to the east stood the treeless home place, its buildings squat under the vast sky. There were the plodding oxen, and his father guiding the plow that was turning up fresh furrows to make the broad, encircling firebreak. Beyond grazed the forty head of McNeill cattle.

In his secret game Evan always saved his pet landmark until the last, pretending, because it seemed wonderful to him, that he had never seen it before. First he looked beyond the homestead and the cattle to Gopherville, a small settlement in the timber along Silver Creek. It was five miles away, but in the clear, dry air Evan could see the curl of smoke and the shape of roofs and chimneys lifted against trees. His gaze veered to the north, where, farther still, another grove thrust its wedge into the prairie. In the middle distance the heads and shoulders of three deer

* This chapter based on the story "Seek No Further," which appeared in Story Parade Magazine. Copyright, 1943, by Mabel Leigh Hunt.

moved through the flowery meadow. Going back in a half circle, past home and Gopherville and around to the south, there was nothing but the tossing grass.

Almost slyly, now, Evan turned toward the west. He gave his chest a companionable thump. "Hey, there 'tis," he reminded the secret Evan McNeill who lived within his twelve-year-old self. Ah, yes, there it was—the magical tree! Alone it stood, king of the prairie. Above the airy billows of the grass, and at nine miles distance, it seemed airy, too, yet with a strength and majesty that had long stirred Evan's imagination. He had never been much nearer to it than at this moment.

If only he had a pony of his own! But he was not even allowed to ride his father's *Hunter*, and eighteen miles of pushing there and back through the thick grass on his own two feet would be hard going. Evan sighed.

"Where've you been, Evan McNeill?" complained six-year-old Janie, when he returned to the cabin. "I called and called you."

"Nowhere p'ticular," answered Evan. His mother turned and smiled at him. Suddenly he wanted to talk to her about the tree. He jerked his thumb over his shoulder. "How do you s'pose that tree ever grew there, all by itself?"

His mother placed her hand on his shoulder. They stood together, looking off across the shimmering miles to the west. "I've often wondered myself, son," she answered. "Your father's been close to it. He says it's an oak. Maybe an Indian dropped an acorn there long ago. Indeed, it's wonderful!"

"But how do you suppose it ever missed getting blown down when it was a sapling, or burned up in a prairie fire?" Evan persisted.

"I couldn't tell you, boy. Maybe it was spared to give you and me something to dream about." For Evan's mother had often seen him gazing into the distance. Now, after a moment's silence, her hand tightened on his shoulder. "Evan McNeill, you and I are going to visit that tree," she announced.

Evan looked up at her quickly. "When?" he asked.

"Tomorrow. Long enough we've been aching to go."

"How shall we get there?" Evan couldn't quite believe it.

"We'll ride Hunter," answered Mother. "I'll fix it up with your father."

She waited until the end of the noonday meal. "Evan and I have got a hankering," she began gravely. "It's a tree-hankering, and there's only one cure for it. Tomorrow we ride to see the lone oak."

"I've got a hankering, too," begged Janie. "I want to go along."

"Yours is only a craving to gallivant, Janie dear," said Mother, smiling. " 'Tisn't the same as what ails Evan and me. We're going, just the two of us, riding Hunter.

Grandma will take care of you and Father, won't you, Ma?"

"I'd hate to think I couldn't look after a man and one child for a day," said Grandma, crisply. "Raised ten young 'uns myself. You and Evan go, Ellie. It'll do you good."

"Hunter's full of spirit," objected Robert McNeill. "He shies at a rabbit. Out there on the prairie he's likely to throw you. And you can see a passel o' trees at Silver Creek, and not go half so far."

"I know," answered Mother, patiently. "The trees are lovely at Silver Creek. But they grew up through the marsh without any trouble, and with plenty of company. The lone oak away off yonder—it's a rare brave thing, pushing up by itself, stubborn and strong, meaning through all its years of growing and reaching to be the best of its kind. Evan and I, we've got to go over and touch it, and look at it, and *think* about it." Mother's lips trembled a little. "As for Hunter," she went on, with sudden spirit, "I can ride him almost as well as you can, Robert."

What a mother for a boy to have! Evan was up very early the next day. It was hard to wait until the morning chores were done, and a lunch packed. "If the buttermilk clabbers in the heat, it won't harm us, and 'twill quench our thirst," laughed Mother. She was as gay as a girl going to her first dance.

"Don't get reckless and ride on to St. Louis," advised Father. "It's about seventy miles due west of the oak." Father was joking, but Evan knew he considered this journey just a foolish notion.

Across the prairie rode Evan and Mother. The June grasses brushed against Hunter's flanks, against Evan's bare feet and the flowing skirt of Mother's riding habit. Spot, one of the dogs followed, flushing quail and prairie chickens and pheasants. Rabbits and field mice scurried here and there. Gophers and badgers ducked into their burrows. Dipping and curving, the field sparrows and meadow larks made sweet music. The soft southwest wind ruffled the grass into waves, now rose, now green. Once the travelers came upon a patch of wild strawberries. "On our way back, we'll fill our empty lunch basket," promised Mother. "I'll make a pie."

"Um-m-m!" murmured Evan, his mouth watering.

But whatever new thing may have claimed their attention, the two never lost sight of their goal. The leafy top of the oak grew broader as they pushed steadily westward. At last Mother pulled on Hunter's reins. They had reached the tree.

"*Whillikens!*" breathed Evan. The oak was more superb than he had guessed it would be. For how many, many years had it drawn through root and trunk the boundless fertility of prairie loam? Now it towered some one hundred and fifty feet in height. Evan's heartbeat was quick as he slipped off the horse. With happy excitement he and Mother stretched arms wide to pass the tethering rope about the massive trunk, tying it securely, that Hunter might not stray. Their hands lingered on the thick, rough ridges of bark. Evan saw tears in his mother's eyes as she looked up at the noble green branches.

They spread their lunch under that cool-shadowing canopy, eating slowly, with scarcely a word spoken, but smiling at one another in deep content. And when they had thrown the scraps to Spot, Mother leaned back against the oak's trunk, and told of the trees of her childhood. Evan realized, then, how hungry she had long been for their green companionship. "The ones I liked best were the apple trees in my father's orchard in York state," said Mother. "In the Spring—oh, the fragrance and beauty of their blossoms! There's something about an apple—well, I think it's a fruit that belongs especially to girls and boys. You, my poor Evan, can only guess what an orchard, or an orchard apple is like.

"I remember that one tree bore apples which we called *Seek-no-furthers*. When they were ripe, some would fall on the house roof where it sloped at the back. *Thump, roll, tumble*—such a merry sound! I can hear it yet."

"Seek-no-further?" echoed Evan, his brow puckered. "Oh, of course," he said at last. "The name described apples so good there was no need to seek further for better ones."

"That's right," said Mother, and she sighed. "Oh, to taste one again!"

When the time came to start homeward, Evan said, "D'you know, Mother, I think this oak might be called *Seek-no-further*, too, because there couldn't be another tree so fine, surely. Besides, Mother, now that I know just how it looks, I shan't be so—well, so hankering to— to *seek* it."

It was easier to share the tiny sweet strawberries with the family that evening than the memory of the day and the tree. And when the milking was done, the stock penned for the night, and the dogs turned out to warn the wolves against preying on his pigs and chickens, Robert McNeill began speaking, slowly. He spoke as if he had been thinking deeply all day. He had something he wanted to say to Mother and Evan. "The forest is itself. The orchard is itself," he said. "And the prairie is itself. I'll take the prairie. I like it just as it is. A man feels like a king in the wide space, under the open sky, here in Illinois. Land like ours is the highest, the most level, the most fertile, although few have had the courage to settle on it. In time they will come away from the trees that grow by the watercourses and breed the ague."

"Ellie," said Grandma, her eyes impish, "Robert's sticking up for the prairie because his conscience pricks him. After you left this morning, I told him he should plant

some trees for Ellie McNeill that had such a hankering for
'em."

Father looked a little sheepish as he laughed and said,
"I'll sow you a grove of locust tree seeds, Ellie. They'll
grow into tall trees in no time. This prairie soil beats
everything for richness."

"I like it on the prairie, too, Robert," said Mother, gently. "It will still be prairie, but lovelier, when we have
the locust grove."

But his stock, his grain and his hunting kept Robert
McNeill very busy. He seemed to forget about the locust
seeds. And Mother was no woman to nag a man. The
prairie grasses deepened to red and to yellow, and finally,
to the brilliant gold of autumn. Then in the crystal air
the lone oak seemed to draw nearer. Evan could almost distinguish its ruddy color. After Indian summer
it was blotted out in the long-falling veils of rain that beat
down the grass and filled up old buffalo wallows and the
dry sloughs. Swirling curtains of snow hid it completely,
but on certain clear winter days Evan could see it, a delicate penciling of bare boughs against the sky.

When Spring brought the prairie to life again with a
green like young wheat, Mother was ailing. Evan and
Janie had to help Grandma with the household chores.
One day Evan was sent to mail an important letter at the
post office in Gopherville. He must walk the five miles.

" 'Tain't bad going," he confided to Grandma, "but coming back it's about twice as long."

Grandma gave him a sharp look. "Never mind about that, Evan," she said. "When folks speak to you over there, hold up your head and answer cordial, as a McNeill should. You'd enjoy yourself more if you weren't so almighty bashful."

Evan flushed. He went without answering. When his errand was done in Gopherville he did have a craving to linger and talk, if only he could think of something neighborly to say. At the same time he was longing to be back on the prairie, where he felt so free and easy. "Guess I'll meander along the creek, first. Maybe there'll be some violets I can pick for Mother. Wish I had something nice to take her—something she wants real bad."

When he came out of the general store and post office, Evan saw a crowd of children. They were dancing alongside a lean, rangy old fellow, hanging to his hands and his shabby coat tails. His gray hair straggled to his shoulders. On his head was a pasteboard hat, the brim cut to form a broad front peak. His clothes were queer. Nothing matched. While Evan stared in curiosity the man seated himself on a grassy bank, the children grouped eagerly about him.

A boy came out of the store. He flung a look at Evan. "That's Johnny Appleseed," he said, answering the question in Evan's eyes. "Come on if you want to hear one of his thunderin' good stories." Evan hesitated, stumbled forward, catching up with the strange boy. "Appleseed—Johnny Appleseed," he stammered, "why is he called that?"

"Why, apple seeds and a place to plant 'em—that's his business," came the ready answer. "But not for money. *Lawzy*, one look at 'im will tell you that!"

Evan caught his breath. "You mean he doesn't want any money for his apple seeds?"

"Oh, if you've got it easy in your pocket, maybe. But he'd just as lief have an old coat, or a shirt, or a bit of corn meal. Or, for that matter, nothing at all."

"Is he going to live in Gopherville?" asked Evan. He had never heard of Johnny Appleseed.

"Naw, 'course not. He says he's bound for St. Louis and the Mississippi."

Evan hung bashfully on the fringe of Johnny's audience. But his mind darted all around the planter's story, although it was a thrilling account of an Ohio hunter's adventure with a bear. *Those apple seeds that could be had in trifling exchange! Or, for nothing!* There was something Evan *must* know about them. When the story was finished and Johnny had gently shaken himself free of the children, Evan followed that long, loping stride, fighting against his shyness. "Mister Appleseed! J—Johnny Appleseed!" he called, at last. "What kind of apples are them you plant? What's the name of 'em?"

Johnny turned and looked into eyes as dark and burning as his own. "Why, lad," he answered, "they're all kinds. *Rambos* and *Seek-no-furthers* and *Fall Wines* and *Golden Pippins* and—well, it doesn't make much difference. An apple is the sweetest and best of all God's fruits, whatever its name."

"It would make a difference to my mother," declared Evan, earnestly, "because she's got a craving for the *Seek-no-furthers* she remembers from a long time back. And I'm asking you, sir," stammered Evan, very red, "if you would stop and talk to my mother about apples on your way to St. Louis. We live off yonder on the prairie. And —maybe—you do have some apple seeds left, don't you?"

"Of course I do," the planter assured Evan, heartily. "God willing, and Johnny Appleseed to do His will, there shall be orchards along the Mississippi. For your mother, too, boy."

"When will you come?" asked Evan.

"I'm ready, now," Johnny answered. "If you'll wait until I get my horse and my seed bags, we'll go together."

Evan was never to forget that journey homeward. "I picked up this gray mare," Johnny explained, "so worn out with travel she was left by the wayside by some westward-going folks to fend for herself. I named her Gillyflower, for the apple. Pretty name, ain't it?" Johnny patted the mare, affectionately. "I've fattened her up since I've had her."

Evan almost laughed, for he could have counted Gilly-flower's ribs. "Are we going to ride?" he asked, hopefully.

"No, lad," answered Johnny. "We're as able to walk as she is, and better. We'll burden her only with my few belongings." Johnny's bushel-bags of seeds were strapped to the mare's back, also his hoe. From the strap hung his kettle and cooking pan. *Tinkle, clink*—with Gillyflower's every step they made a harsh, humorous music. Johnny talked. His voice had the wilderness in it, but gentle, so that Evan completely forgot his shyness. When the cabin was reached, he introduced his companion with rare pride.

"Welcome, Johnny Appleseed," said Father. "I've heard of you."

"Mother," whispered Evan, "he's got all kinds of apple seeds."

"I'll plant you an orchard, ma'am," Johnny spoke up. "There ought to be some *Seek-no-further* trees among them to give you extra pleasure."

"I'll let you have a plot of ground close to the house, Johnny," promised Father.

"He was saving it for a locust grove," explained Grandma, and she stole a sly look at Father. "Gave Ellie hope of it 'most a year ago."

"We'll have both," Father said. "There's plenty of room for both."

"I declare!" sighed Mother, happily. "Apple *and* locust trees!"

Evan was proud when Father said, "Thanks to you, son, for bringing Johnny Appleseed to us."

"For once Evan spoke up in Gopherville like a McNeill should," chuckled Grandma. "But I guess it was because he wanted to bring Ellie something nice."

Evan helped the planter prepare the soil and sow the seeds. He listened carefully to Johnny's instructions; how to water the young seedlings through the blazing summer; how to protect them with wrappings of dried grass and cornstalks from winter frosts and the nibbling of rabbits. Father hauled fencing from Gopherville. Mother grew well and strong again. Grandma said it was because of the tonic of mullein leaves and milk which Johnny brewed for her. Deep in his mind, Evan thought it was the promise of apple bloom.

Johnny lent a hard hand to the chores. He made a cradle for Janie's doll. He told her about other little girls he had known—Nancy Metzger and Megan McIlvain: Rosella Rice of the lovely Mohican valley: Eliza Rudisill of Fort Wayne. His eyes shone as he told Janie of his nieces, the Brooms, who, when they were little, "could kite up the peg ladder that led to the loft of their cabin home, like squirrels." The McNeill family listened spellbound to his stories of settlers and Indians. Through all his talk ran, like a silver thread, the flow of the western watercourses, and Johnny following creek and river to sow his apple seeds in some waiting plot. At bedtime he read from his tattered Bible. He slept on the floor, his thin gray locks falling about his shoulders, his weathered cheek resting on his palm.

From the master of the house to the scrubbiest dog, everyone loved him. When he said he must go, Janie shed tears. "Johnny, how you have blessed our house and fields!" cried Grandma. And Father, his hand on Johnny's shoulder, advised him. "Man, it's amazing to think how many nurseries you've planted in the West. Isn't it time to take your ease? Johnny, don't go on. Stay here with us. You're getting old."

"Must be nearing the last of my sixties," Johnny answered, smiling. "But I'm still able, and my work not done. Besides, for an enduring time I've been cur'us to see where all the little cricks and runs and rivers of Ohio and Indiana and Illinois are bound for. Well, I know they're bound for the Mississippi, and so am I." The way Johnny said it, didn't it sound like a refrain, with perhaps a twangy little tune to it, altogether joyous?

O, they're going to the Mississippi,
And so am I, so am I!

Evan and Mother rode across the prairie with Johnny as far as the lone oak. Evan felt no sadness. Indeed, it seemed to him he had never been happier. He chattered and he whistled. He stood on his head. He turned cartwheels all around the oak. "I declare, Evan," laughed his mother, "have you gone witless?"

"It's only that the boy is full of youth, the springtide, and the thought of an orchard full of apples," offered Johnny.

"*Seek-no-furthers*," Evan reminded him.

"Remember, lad," Johnny said, "*Seek-no-further* is a mighty fine name for an apple, or for an oak. But 'seek further' would be a better motto for a boy."

Evan was thoughtful as he and his mother watched the old apple missionary and the nag Gillyflower plodding westward.

"There's no real sorrow in saying good-by to Johnny," said Mother, quietly, "for we know that wherever he goes he will leave such promise as he has left with us. He may not be great, but a man whose trace shall last as long in beauty and bounty as Johnny's, a man who plants for the future good of mankind in the way he can plant best, has greatness in him."

"I guess that's what he meant," answered Evan, "when he said I should be a *seek-further* one, as Johnny has always been." One hand resting on the great trunk of the oak, Evan's voice rang out over the prairie. "Good-by, Johnny Appleseed." Johnny turned, waving a last farewell.

> O, we're going to the Mississippi,
> The rivers and I, the rivers and I.
> Good-by to all, good-by, good-by-y-y.

Part III
THE HARVEST

VIII. ORCHARDS
IN THE VALLEYS

THERE was a little Swedenborgian "temple" in Cincinnati. Adam Hurdus was pastor, and his sermons were so lengthy as to give a man time to fall into a comfortable doze. But if that man happened to be a certain visiting New-church missionary, he had no desire to sleep. Johnny Appleseed, listening with rapt attention, stored away in his mind nuggets of convincing doctrine for use in the arguments he loved to hold with friends and strangers from Lake Erie to the Ohio, from the Tuscarawas to the Wabash.

If Johnny had a mind to—and he had—he could stay in the temple the entire Sabbath, except for the intermissions between services. Munching his corn dodgers, he was eager to take his seat again. For besides the sermon, there was the psalmody, and Johnny singing *Old Hundred* and *Vital Spark* as lustily as anyone, to the accompaniment of the organ which Adam Hurdus had built with his own hands. A marvel, that—and played very well by young

179

Sol Smith, who, when he was not in Cincinnati conducting the New Jerusalem Singing Society, roved over the country as a "stage-actor," and sang, instead of hymns, such worldly ballads as *Bay of Biscay*, and *Oh, my luve's like a red, red rose.*

Crikey, did Johnny tread barefoot into the temple, wearing his sackcloth garment and his tattered pantaloons? Or had he, in exchange for some apple trees, diked himself out in passable boots and a rusty cloth coat? In the forest a man could talk with the angels—departed kin and friends—and never did they mind how he was clad. But in Cincinnati, perhaps Johnny was willing to put on a little style to honor God's temple, the good Mr. Hurdus, the wonderful organ, and the New-church congregation in its best bib and tucker.

But alas, try as we may, we cannot spruce up Johnny Appleseed. He remains forever the saintly, bright-eyed scarecrow. He wore whatever garments he happened to possess at the moment. They were always poor, generally second-hand. In his humility he wished to go no finer than the neediest of his fellow men. Without sanctimony he wished to follow the scriptural injunction to "provide... for your journey neither two coats, neither shoes—"

In Cincinnati Johnny was welcomed by his friends the Ecksteins. Their son-in-law, Alexander Kinmont, was a brilliant scholar and teacher. He was also a most devout and learned Swedenborgian. Johnny Appleseed was ever

quick to take advantage of the interpretation of Swedenborgian writings which such educated men as Hurdus and
Kinmont could give him. In his rambles he reflected upon
all he had been told and that which he read from his own
pack of literature.

Leaf mold and pine needles are more agreeable to a pilgrim's feet than cobblestones, and Johnny felt not at home
in cities. With many steamboats docking at its wide new
wharf and its residences beginning to spread upward
among the hills, Cincinnati was at this time the largest city
in the West. But before he left it, Johnny collected seeds
from its big apple, peach and plum orchards.

His supplies replenished, his soul refreshed, Johnny
struck up through Mill Creek Valley to reach his old nursery along Wayne's War Road, where the fathers of Ohio
had established the first state university long ago. Directly
west was Lebanon, which nurtured a society of Swedenborgians. Johnny must exchange some good talk with its
members. Urbana-bound, he could have stopped at another nursery, or the site of it, on the Shawnee trail above
Old Town, an Indian village rich in historic lore. In 1826
the National Pike, now as far as Zanesville, was crawling
forward to bring immense growth to Springfield. It would
swallow up that old nursery of Johnny Appleseed's.

All along his journey he heard excited talk about the
building of the Miami and Erie canal, now under way. It
was still a subject as touchy as a hot potato, the more pro-

gressive trying to convince the die-hards that a canal system would lift Ohio right out of its pioneer cradle into a new era of growth. Johnny believed in growth. Was he not, in his fashion, doing all he could for it? But he felt a little sadness, also. The time was surely coming when his work would no longer be needed in Ohio.

At Urbana, Johnny sought legal advice in the office of John H. James. He had respect for the law, and considering what a *John-the-Baptist* sort of fellow Johnny Appleseed was, it seems rather delightful to know that so many of his friends were "Honorables"—the Judges Wetmore and Young in Pennsylvania, and here in Ohio, the Honorables Bartley, Stanberry, James, and others. In reminiscence they always spoke well of him. He was so eccentric as to interest and amuse them, but it is probable that they also found him disarming and lovable because of his rustic simplicity and goodness. Said the Honorable James:

In 1826 ... he came to my office ... bearing a letter from ... Alexander Kinmont. It stated that ... some years before he [Johnny] *had planted on the land of a person who gave him leave. Afterward the land was sold. Johnny had been told that the present owner might not recognize his right to the trees. He did not seem anxious, however. He continued walking to and fro as he talked, eating nuts. I advised him ... to see the owner of the land ... He was of medium height, very coarsely clad and his costume carelessly worn.*

One can imagine the judge tipping back his chair and putting his feet up on his desk, drawing Johnny out in conversation. The planter was soon eagerly holding forth on his favorite subjects of apples and religion, for the judge related afterward how decidedly his visitor spoke against grafting, and that "the proper method was to raise trees from seed." The judge went on: *All I know of the Swedenborgian religion I learned from Johnny Appleseed.*

Leaving Urbana, it would have been a pity for Johnny not to strike across country for a little visit in Worthington. There his friend Ezra Griswold kept a beautiful seventeen-room brick tavern, with a great arched gate cut in one wall, through which the wheeled and the mounted might ride to an inner court. Ezra's inn still stands in that lovely town, and his descendants point smilingly to the wide fireplace, at whose warmth Johnny slept more than once, so they say.

Familiar ground and old friends beckoned to him from near Delaware, and since he believed so fervently that man should accept with gratitude the gifts of Nature, Johnny would have made it a point to drink from the sulphur springs at this place. His haunts in Crawford County now lay due north. Of course he must see how George Gill was getting along, and his orchard, grown from Johnny's saplings, which was to become one of Galion's landmarks on Gill Avenue.

At the Wyandot reservation, at Upper Sandusky, the rover might have stopped to rest and give the Indians religious counsel. Within a day or two, perhaps he went on to Hancock County. In 1826 it was still so thinly settled that only twenty-six taxpayers were registered. In time it became a matter of guesswork among the county folk as to how long ago Johnny had cleared and sowed the river bottoms eight miles downstream from Findlay. They wondered if it had been the red men or Johnny Appleseed who planted the "Plum-orchard" near the old burying ground. Whether or not Johnny visited it in 1826, he came again about 1840. Was it in Spring, when the air was laden with the fragrance of plum blossom, or was it deep Summer, and Johnny lying indolently among the old Indian mounds, munching the mellow fruit with relish and contentment? One who saw him in Findlay said: *He was quite an old man, and did not appear to have a very great quantity of this world's goods. He was regarded as intelligent ...but slightly demented...* (He) *was full of pleasant story, and good advice after his fashion.*

In 1828, Johnny sold one of the three lots he had bought nineteen years before in Mount Vernon, for which he had paid Joseph Walker a total of fifty dollars. Property had increased in value, and Johnny the gainer, as can be seen in the terms of the deed, still on file in the recorder's office in Knox County:

John Chapman, to Jesse B. Thomas:
Know all men by these presents, that I, John Chapman (by occupation a gatherer and planter of apple seeds) residing in Richland County, for the sum of thirty dollars, honest money, do hereby grant to said Jesse B. Thomas, late Senator from Illinois, his heirs and assigns forever, Lot No. 145, in the corporation limits of the village of Mt. Vernon, State of Ohio.

Heigh-ho! For all of Johnny's wanderings he still called Richland County "home!" Ah, yes, wasn't he forever plodding back, to exchange pleasant greetings and reminiscences; to gloat over the productive orchards and savor their fruit; to delve into his story bag for the delight of children? Once he himself organized a Swedenborgian Society there. Five or six families joined. But what with life being so hard and so intensely practical, and Johnny being away so much, it seemed as if the members failed to put their understanding to it, although in occasional night-broodings they must have sometimes yearned for it, remembering how, when Johnny had talked of it, they came near to catching a glimpse of Paradise.

From Mount Vernon and Mansfield to the Maumee valley is a long way to go by foot. But what were the miles to Johnny Appleseed? While he already knew parts of the valley along the lower Auglaize, and had his special friends at Shane's Crossing on the St. Mary's River, at some time during the latter half of the 1820's Johnny again sallied forth for the northwest. It remained the wildest of Ohio's lands—country which had become hers by terms of the treaty made with the Indians at St. Mary's in 1818. Only since the signing had white settlers begun to locate there, for the Indians held large reservations, and it would take years to clear the mammoth forests and drain the vast muck of the Black Swamp, impenetrable and reeking with malaria. But what with the coming canal boom, and the certainty that the government would buy off every last Indian and send him to the far West, this wilderness would be cleared and settled. Was not "a gatherer and planter of apple seeds" beholden to sow the Maumee valley?

Now in this land there flourished old apple trees which were thought to have been planted by French missionaries and traders. They had been discovered growing near Indian trading posts and villages by American soldiers and first settlers. And whether the age of the trees and the mystery of their planting made them heroic in men's eyes, the story goes that they were of immense size and fabulous fruitfulness. In Johnny's day those at the Defiance settlement were already legendary.

Hearing about the trees, Johnny would have traveled far to see them, and to take the seeds from their fruit. In 1828, when he came to Defiance, where below the bluff the Auglaize and Maumee rivers met in beautiful con-

fluence, Johnny saw for himself the row of giants growing as tall as forest trees along the brimming Auglaize. But
the sight of those which stood on the north bank of the
Maumee took Johnny's breath. One in particular was a
show piece. Defiance pointed to it with pride, and travelers gaped at its girth and height. In the springtime, this
stalwart old mother tree became a girl again, her head
crowned with myriad blossoms, and all the air, even bluff-
high at the fort, was filled with perfume. The wild bees
came. The petals fell, one by one, drifting down the river.
The baby apples grew and ripened in summer's gracious
warmth. The fruit was gathered by the bushel—enough
for all—Indian, white settler, wayfarer. Today a marker,
dated 1670–1887, shows where that famous French-Indian
Apple Tree once stood.

Oh, but Johnny Appleseed must plant in loam so deep
as to nurture such lasting abundance! He trekked a mile
up the Auglaize from Defiance to the mouth of the Tiffin
River, and started a nursery near what is now Brunersburg.
The yarn spinners said that he lived, with room enough
and to spare, in a hollow sycamore, for the tree was thirteen feet thick, so they declared. Several thousand saplings
sprouted from Johnny's sowing on the Tiffin. In about
two years he took them up (at what labor!) and trans-
planted them to cleared land near the present Florida, in
Henry County. This land lies along the upper Maumee as
it flows to Lake Erie. The astute Johnny knew that cabins

would spring up to face the canal which was to parallel the river. There must be apple trees at those cabin doors. And, indeed, until his seedlings were finally sold out from this nursery, it supplied orchards all through the valley.

In Defiance stands a marker to Johnny Appleseed, too. It names him—*Benefactor*.

1830-1845

IX. AT THE MEETING
OF RIVERS

THERE is a trail leading into Indiana. But it is very lonely, wolf-infested. Not a single house, it is said, between Defiance and Fort Wayne. Then follow the river, Johnny Appleseed. It twists and turns in erratic caprice which will lengthen your journey. Too, you must push against the current. Your craft is nothing more than a clumsy dugout, the hollowed-out section of a log. The Indian or the trader in his sleek canoe overtakes and passes you. The long pirogue launched at Fort Defiance, with its passengers seated one behind the other, glides swiftly by. When night falls they, as well as you, must go ashore and make camp, for the distance by water is over a hundred miles. But there is no fret of hurry in you. Perhaps you sing as you dip your paddles. It is singing weather, the sky as blue as a bluebird's feather, and every autumn-bright tree along the shores a pillar of praise. Perhaps, as the colored leaves drift down among your seed bags, you repeat aloud the harmony of the Beatitudes, which dwell in your mind as favorite tunes dwell in the mind of a song maker. *Blessed are the poor in spirit; for their's is the kingdom of heaven...Blessed are the meek; for they shall inherit the earth.*

So this was the Maumee River, born of the union between the St. Mary's and the St. Joseph, in the heart of Fort Wayne. This was the autumn of 1830, and time that Johnny Appleseed was on his way. With that remarkable foresight which advised him when and where to plant, Johnny knew that it was time.

It was time because the country was on the verge of a new era. It was time because Fort Wayne had recently attained the stature of an incorporated town. The population was not more than four hundred: the forest crowded up to the very doors. A man might live—yes, and die—in the neighboring forest, and none in the village the wiser. But those who were setting up their stores and mills and taverns—Ewing and Swinney, Allen and Hanna and Tabor—every resident from judge to cobbler, held confident visions of a city. Why not? The newcomers who arrived by river or trail were of a substantial type. They had real money in their pockets. They were land hungry. For was not the surveying being done for building the Wabash and Erie canal? The first spadeful of earth would be lifted at Fort Wayne. There would be a scramble for lands along its route. New settlement, expansion! By that time Johnny Appleseed's saplings would be ready to sell and transplant to newly cleared farms. With this certainty of vision clear in his mind, he concluded his voyage, and tied up at the landing place below the old fort.

Curious fellow, he appeared no better than a beggar! On one foot was an old shoe tied on with strings, on the other a boot which had seen better days. He wore a pyramid of three hats, so-called. The first was only a brim. Next came his cooking pot. Surmounting all was a hat with a crown. The sum total was, if extremely odd, rather ingenious. It enabled Johnny to carry not only his kettle, but his treasure of sacred literature, sandwiched between the pot and the crown of the uppermost hat. The books were kept dry, and Johnny's hands left free to deal with seed bags and tools.

However, the citizens of Fort Wayne were accustomed to a great variety of arrivals, and in numbers. Indeed, men had been breasting the Maumee ever since the first travelers had discovered that this Indian village marked the only break in a water route that proved the shortest distance between the mouth of the St. Lawrence and that of the Mississippi. Follow that route, and a pirogue need never be lifted from the water save for a seven-mile portage from the village southwest to the Little Wabash. Consequently, Fort Wayne had become the focus and center of communication and trade for as long as tribes and nations had found it and coveted it and shed blood for its possession and control of the portage. To the Indians of Ohio and Indiana it was still Kekionga—*Meeting of the Ways*, heart of the Miami nation. The French-Canadians and half-breeds were apt to call it Miami town. To the Americans it was Fort Wayne, named for that dauntless "Mad Anthony" who had won it for America. During the next fifteen years Johnny Appleseed was to know it well.

Where did he sleep that first night in Fort Wayne? Curled up in his dugout like a fox? Or perhaps he lay on the barroom floor of Washington Hall, Mr. Ewing's tavern, or in the cabin of the Quaker, William Worth, formerly of Ohio. He may already have become acquainted with Fort Wayne, for he knew Indiana before it became a state in 1816. He had planted, so it is said, along the Ohio river borders, and in the Whitewater valley near Richmond. From there he could have followed the Quaker trace to Fort Wayne. Or he could have reached it by way of the St. Mary's River from his nursery at Shanesville, in Ohio. It would have been a jaunt of but thirty miles had he decided to look the settlement over while visiting his half sister Persis, for the Brooms had located, prior to 1830, on a farm in Indiana's Jay County. In fact, it seems probable that Johnny preceded the Brooms and induced them to emigrate to his planting near the present village of New Corydon. Print records that he was one of Jay County's pioneers, *having brought, on the back of an ox, two bushels of apple seeds, which he planted in various places.* Whatever may be true, it seems that in this autumn of Johnny's fifty-sixth year, he was buying or leasing acreage at Fort Wayne's land office. Next, he was sowing seeds thereon, east of the village along the Maumee, near the spot where the canal lock would one day lift the first packet-boat from one level to another. He planted a second plot near the village along the same river, and not long afterward floated downstream several miles and started a nursery of fifteen thousand trees.

There was an Indian trail leading north out of Fort Wayne, which eventually passed along the eastern edge of Elkhart Prairie, to the present town of Goshen. Perhaps the grasses of wide Elkhart, softly swaying in April air and melodious with April song, seemed lovely to Johnny Appleseed when he came in the springtide and planted along the bottoms of the Elkhart River. The Miamis and the Pottawatomies were sowing their fields along the prairie borders, north and south. One can imagine missionary Johnny earnestly trying to convince them that the paths of righteousness may lead to a land more beautiful than a prairie in Spring.

So for months Johnny went about his business, plant-

ing in northern Indiana and lower Michigan localities
which were attracting settlers. But whenever he returned
to Fort Wayne, he saw changes, and to match its growth,
started additional nurseries on the St. Mary's and the St.
Joseph. Besides his friend Worth, he had other favorites.
Among them was Benjamin Archer, a farmer and brick-
maker north of town, and Captain Henry Rudisill, who
ran a gristmill on the St. Joseph. At Rudisill's mill Johnny
could scrape up any chance leavings of meal for his mush
pot. He could argue religion with Henry, who was a
Lutheran. Too, Johnny loved and told stories to Eliza,
Captain Henry's little daughter. Sometimes, at night,
when Johnny chanced to be at the Rudisill home, he
would call the child's attention to the glory of the stars.
As the two gazed upward, Johnny would let fall strange
remarks which Eliza could not understand, but which
ever afterward shimmered in her mind like stardust. Perhaps Johnny bought this little maid a red ribbon on that
Washington's Birthday of 1840 when he purchased a
pocketknife on credit at Hamilton and Tabor's trading
store. He paid the debt of seventy-five cents the following
April. The record of that transaction with "John Appleseed" may be seen today in the old account book owned
by the joint local historical societies at Fort Wayne.

Johnny saw the growing town in all its picturesque
contrasts. Until 1837 the streets were full of water holes
and thickets of underbrush. But the first courthouse lifted

itself importantly in the "Publick Square" in 1832: the first issue of the *Fort Wayne Sentinel* came damp from the little press in 1833, and the next year the first bank was established. Everyone from the wealthiest merchant-trader to Johnny Appleseed drank from the same tin cup at the village pump. A crude town of logs, yet a riot of roses covering the double-hewn residence of Major Lewis; and each citizen and visitor coming to admire the flowers in their lavish June heyday.

On Columbia and Barr streets might be seen the blankets and feathered turbans of Indian men; the brooches and tinkling ear-bobs of the Miami belles. There were the red shirts of the Canadians, the hunters' buckskins, and the linsey-woolseys. On grand occasions might be seen the elegant frock coats and snowy shirt bosoms of gentlemen merchants. At a wedding in the old fort the bride wore a gown of heliotrope brocade.

Hundreds of Indians from the reservations thronged the town on trading days, or when they came to receive their government annuities. Traders from far and near gathered to ply them with liquor, to trick and rob them —a high old time of drinking and whooping, horse racing and gambling. Sometimes the militia had to be called out to quell the riots. Yet the dignified nieces of the great war chief Little Turtle, dropped substantial and pious offerings into the church's collection basket. And of all the smaller dramas enacted in the pageantry of old Fort

Wayne, none is prettier than that of Chief Richardville, prince of the Miami nation, coming up from his reservation to see that no harm had befallen the apple tree which marked his birthplace in the village. Perhaps the tree brought Richardville and Johnny together in pleasant apple-ish conversation; Johnny threadbare, the Indian prince in his costly, fantastic finery. Ah, but the chief was very rich, and kept his money in an iron-bound safe at the handsome brick house the government had built for him! He had his Turkey carpets and damask curtains, and servants to wait upon him. He carried on an immense trade, importing his goods from far places. But his sentiment for the apple tree of his childhood was as honest and tender as the earth which nurtured it. A portrayal of the many picturesque characters familiar to Fort Wayne in those days would paint a glowing canvas.

February 22nd, 1832. Bonfires leaped skyward. All of Fort Wayne stepped high in parade. A candle shone in every window, proclaiming that work had started on the long-awaited canal. A horde of brawny Irish roared into the valley to dig "the big ditch." Sure, now, and weren't they the wild ones, throwing their weight around, and their jokes and their songs? And wasn't it a hullabaloo when the men of Cork lit into the Fardown men, tooth and nail, and the Fardownians made mincemeat of the Corkonians? The feud was so dreadful folks called it "the Irish war!" In 1835, the northern division of the canal was

opened for navigation. The people went wild with excitement. Artillery and oratory boomed. Thirty-three young
ladies paraded, each representing a state of the glorious
Union. Presently, the *Indiana,* the first packet, was towed
along the brimming channel. Other boats were built and
floated, one of them named the *Chief Richardville.* Oh,
the exciting new times—America growing up, growing
fast—and a rejoicing in every heart, a cheer in every
throat, and from many a wallet the new paper money
pouring out to swell a dangerous inflation. The crash came
in 1837.

In 1840, during the "Hard-cider" presidential cam-
paign, all this western country became a bedlam of politi-
cal frenzy. It sang and yelled itself hoarse. It rode on
countless log-cabin floats. The torchlights flared. The
bonfires roared. Girls wore buckeye necklaces: men
twirled buckeye canes, because William Henry Harrison, the Whig candidate, was a native of Ohio, the Buckeye state. "Hurrah for Harrison!" bellowed the Whig.
"Hurrah for the devil!" sneered the Democrat. "Every
man hurrah for his own candidate!" was the comeback.
Was Johnny Appleseed a voting man, casting his ballot
in Fort Wayne? Or did he trudge back to Mansfield? It
was said of him that he returned to Richland County every
year.

He took leave of Fort Wayne frequently. He was still
the zealous orchardist. Too, he always preferred the

woods and fields to the towns. He liked the farmer folk. They were both friends and customers. A farmer boy of the region named Ivan Richey knew Johnny, and at ninety-nine spoke of him picturesquely:

He [Johnny] *used to stand around eating apples, but he never threw away the seeds. He'd either pick 'em out and put 'em in his pocket or go to the side of the road and plant them. . . . He and father used to set up . . . till midnight arguing over every subject under the sun, especially religion, and there was where Johnny was perfectly at home. . . . Maybe again during the year he would show up, but he was always welcome, for Father liked him, both for his religion and his interesting conversation. . . . He was widely known and respected among pioneers. . . . One thing Johnny surely did love, and that was corn bread. He always ate his fill. He talked slowish like and used good language. . . . He was quick in action and strong in walking. When he got a little excited his eyes snapped fire. . . .*

Another who knew Johnny in Fort Wayne remembered that *his fine features, seen through the gray stubble that covered his face, told of his intelligence. . . . He must have had money, but he never exhibited any, nor looked as if he had any.*

Hiram Porter was a boy who lived in the same neighborhood as the Worths and Rudisills. Among his reminiscences appears the one dissenting note as to Johnny's ability to read and write:

At one time I wrote a letter for him to a man in Pennsylvania, ordering one-half bushel of apple seeds....He [Johnny] always carried a Testament, for while he had difficulty in reading, he listened to the Scriptures when they were read to him....If he stubbed his toe while walking, he would remove the shoe and go barefoot in order to punish the foot for not performing its duty....He planted a great number of small orchards. Many of these extended along the Wabash River over into Illinois.

So Johnny took the ancient portage out of Fort Wayne and went down into the Wabash country. The river joins the Ohio at Indiana's southwest corner. The Wabash towns knew him. But no one remembered whether he reached the Mississippi by way of the Ohio, or by following the Kankakee and the Illinois. But he came at last to the great stream—the Mississippi, dream river of his old age, as the Ohio had lured his youth!

It is said that Johnny planted in eastern Iowa, where Indian lands had been released and offered for sale. In 1843, a certain Silas Mitchell was living in Whiteside county, Illinois; its western border looks across the Mississippi into Iowa. Silas had known Johnny in Ohio. Writing a letter back to Knox County, he said that Johnny Appleseed had been stopping briefly in the neighborhood, and was on his way to a Swedenborgian convention in Philadelphia. How the imagination revels in that casual

statement! Link it with a certain small reminiscence of a
Fort Wayne old-timer, in which Johnny appears in a
stovepipe hat and a claw hammer coat, and it becomes exciting. Johnny Appleseed a man of style? Johnny going
east by packet or stagecoach, or perhaps indulging himself with a ride on one of the little trains which chugged
along brief stretches of railroad? Fancy Johnny walking
into the temple, pale with exaltation. Fancy him listening
with humility, but surely with pleasure, to praise such as
was given him in a church report in 1822. "What shall be
the reward of such an individual, where, as we are told in
Holy Writ, *They that turn many to righteousness shall
shine as the stars forever.*"

But alas, such delightful visions of Johnny going to the
convention spring from sympathy, not from records.

In 1843 (it could have been 1842 or 1844), Johnny paid
his last visit to Ohio. At that time it had the third largest
population among the states. Railroads and canals, new
roads, spreading towns and tillage—almost gone was the
need for a sower of apple seeds. But Ohio's youth had been
Johnny's youth, and now in his age he walked the land
and saw the fruitage of his labors, the harvest of his years.
Surely it made his heart warm, his step more free, his hope
of heaven brighter. Now in greeting he offered his gnarled
hand to friends and kin from the Tiffin to the Muskingum,
from Lake Erie to the Scioto. There was the same cordial
exchange of talk—religion and apples, people and events:

the stories old and new, and children listening. In content Johnny slept on the welcoming hearthstones of venerable cabins and modern brick dwellings. The days went by, too quickly. The westward-going look, the lifelong resolve, dawned anew in Johnny's eyes. So he said his last farewells, and like an old dog which knows where it is going and why, Johnny returned to Indiana.

The winter was dark. Rain flooded swamps and lowlands. Rain fell in endless weeping, like the weeping of the Indians as they mourned their coming departure for the west. Rain beat down on the new-cut timbers with which Johnny's brother-in-law was building a barn on Johnny's seventy-four acres near the Broom home in Jay County. There was a new cabin. Looked as if the old man were going to stop his traipsing. Looked as if he were going to settle down as an old man should.

Came March, with now and then a breath of Spring, the willow catkins out, among the wet leaves the first green blades shooting up. Johnny felt the familiar urge stirring within him. When the poor Indians were led away, their lands would be open to white settlers. Orchards? Johnny saw them, orderly, fruitful. What if he were in his seventy-second year? He was still hale and hearty. He looked over his store of seeds and mended his sacks. He cleaned the rust from his hoe. If tomorrow were promising—

But snow fell, the deep, clinging snow of March. According to one story, word came to Johnny that cattle had broken into a certain nursery of his in a northern Indiana county. His trees were his children. These injured ones needed him.

On his return, Johnny sought the home of William Worth, on the St. Joseph River. There was an Indian hut on Worth's land, long-abandoned, in which Johnny had often slept. Now he built a fire, and in his old wet clothing, sank down on the ancient hearthstone, gratefully, but sick unto death. He had contracted pneumonia. The neighbors called it the "winter plague."

Johnny had no cozy bed, no linen sheets, no cool pillow under his burning cheek, no clean white bed gown. He received rough and casual kindness; he had shelter; the cup held to the fevered lip; a looking in now and then to see how the poor old man was doing. *Can't help 'im much. The winter plague'll tuck one of us under the sod quicker'n most anything else.*

But Johnny Appleseed was of tough fiber. He lingered. In his rational moments did he fret about his seventeen thousand trees, his lands of almost three hundred fertile acres in Allen and Jay counties? What if he had known it would take the court ten years to settle his estate? Friends and relatives stepped up to declare claims of one kind and another. There were sales transactions, expenses of administration. There were costs of appraisals. (His old gray mare was estimated to be worth $17.50. Today's value of his lands would amount to many thousands of dollars.) All these court proceedings the material after-crop of Johnny's plantings? Perhaps he would have said that nothing of earth mattered now—nothing at all!

Sometimes he heard the swollen river flowing past the hut. Its current seemed to pick him up and bear him swiftly away—to the Ohio and the Monongahela and the Allegheny. He was riding the Susquehanna, a youth in buckskins. He was a boy on the Connecticut, light-headed with the joy of space. He was a little tad in skirts, laughing with the merry brooks of Leominster. And then, in the giddiness of his delirium, he was back on the St. Joseph, struggling, fighting for his breath as the stream rushed him down to the *Meeting of the Ways*, and washed him ashore in old Fort Wayne. He lay there, and peace came to him. No longer was he a suffering old man, dying harshly in an Indian hut. He was young and strong. It was the springtime. He was ready for a new journey. Yonder, leading away from the three rivers, he beheld a new one, a river he had never seen before. It was crystal-bright. He would follow it.

"The old man died last night," so William Worth informed the neighbors.

Four days later, on March 22nd, 1845, the *Fort Wayne Sentinel* printed a notice:

Dies ... in this neighborhood, at an advanced age, Mr.

John Chapman (better known as Johnny Appleseed). The deceased was well known throughout this region by his eccentricity, and (his) strange garb.... He is supposed to have considerable property, yet denied himself almost the common necessities of life—not so much perhaps from avarice as from his peculiar notions on religious subjects. ...He submitted to every privation with cheerfulness and content, believing that in so doing he was securing snug quarters hereafter.... He always carried with him some work on the doctrines of Swedenbough [Swedenborg] *...and would readily converse and argue on his tenets, using much shrewdnes and penetration.... His death was quite sudden. He was seen on our streets a day or two previous.*

Better known as Johnny Appleseed. The phrase appears dim and small in the close-set, old-fashioned type. It is fading away into the very fabric of the aged paper. But look, it grows larger, clearer! It seems to bloom with soft colors, the motley of an old legend—pink and pearl of apple blossom; apple colors in russet and red and yellow; forest green; the silver of the running stream. And, lest the words show bright beyond their due, the dusty old gray of an apple-seed sack.

X. JOHNNY APPLESEED
TRAVELS ON

IT IS mid-May, leaden-skied. The wind blows cold off the St. Joseph River. The people seated on the bleachers snuggle down into their coat collars, shivering. Many of them are residents of Fort Wayne, that teeming modern city which has grown out of old Kekionga, out of old Miami town. Some have come from afar. There are Swedenborgians and horticulturists, city and state officials, historical society and commission members. There are biographers, professors and teachers. Children are here. All are present because they are lovers of a living legend, the life-and-legend of Johnny Appleseed.

The bleachers face the speakers' stand. They face the long esplanade, which is to become part of Fort Wayne's three-hundred-acre Johnny Appleseed Memorial Park, bordering the river. To the right, in the near distance, may be seen the handsome Johnny Appleseed Memorial Bridge, now to be dedicated.

It has been a full day—the morning meeting: the luncheon: the excursion by bus and private car to the unloading place nearest the grave of Johnny Appleseed, now also a part of the Memorial Park.

The old Archer cemetery is a woodsy knoll, quiet, haunted by whispers of the long ago, bright with flowering crab. The people gather around the little fence which guards the grave. The men bare their heads. "We meet here to commemorate"—the services begin. A Swedenborgian minister reads the Twenty-third Psalm from Johnny's own Bible. "He leadeth me beside the still waters.... Yea, though I walk through the valley—" *Oh, Johnny—Johnny Appleseed, might not these words have been sung expressly for you?* The rites continue. A scholarly authority pays tribute to John Chapman as missionary and planter, man and legend. He quotes from Vachel Lindsay, that poet who idolized Johnny the mystic, the poet who understood and interpreted him the most beautifully of all:

> An angel in each apple....
> A ballot-box in each apple,
>
> .   .   .   .   .
>
> All America in each apple....

There is music at the grave, a rollicking chorus sung by merry-eyed little girls. For to children Johnny Appleseed is their very own saint— Joy in droll clothing, scattering the fruits of joy.... A wreath of flowers is placed upon the grave.

And now by the riverside the people wait for the dedicatory address. There are preliminaries. Fort Wayne's mayor speaks of the new park as a symbol of his city's growth and prosperity. A tall high-school lad speaks. He is picturesquely clad in buckskins and a coonskin cap. He has a Yankee look, keen and humorous. It is not too difficult to imagine him as young John Chapman setting out for the West. Only he has not come on foot, but by air, to represent the city of Leominster as Johnny's birthplace.

As he tells of the apple festival held annually in his county back in the old Bay State, and the monument erected on the site of the Chapman home, the listeners call up mental visions of other memorials, such as the stone in the heart of Ashland, Ohio: the quiet, moss-grown shaft in a Mansfield park, and the school bearing his name: the drinking trough at Wellsburg. Throughout the land are the arboretums, orchards and parks, all lovingly laid out and planted in Johnny's honor. And there is that last remaining tree of Johnny's planting in Ashland county, so it is claimed—one relic of that thirty-acre orchard he set out for his friend John Springer, long, long ago.

And are not the tributes of speech memorials, and those of pen and brush and song? Johnny of the film, completely carefree: Johnny manifold and various in play, radio skit, operetta and ballet. Oh, the absurdity of horny-footed, religious old Johnny playing the *merry-andrew* before the footlights! There's the Johnny Appleseed scarcely noticed by historians: there's Johnny gently scorned by the professional fruit-growers, yet they call him an early hero of horticulture, and pay him honor for his unique service to the pioneers.

Johnny—for a moment, on the other side of the river appears a wraith of a figure, an old fellow in scarecrow clothes, and with a pack on his back. A vagabond loitering within sight of the state's highest official and all this well-dressed company? Yet—isn't there some peculiar gentleness about him, something amusing, some shining legendary saintliness? Surely, now—it can't be—

The wandering fancy rests. The mind leaps to attention. For Indiana's governor is rising to his feet. He has laid aside his famous white hat. The chill wind stirs his hair. He speaks earnestly, his theme bearing upon our national heritage—freedom, and our will to work together for the common good, a heritage which Johnny Appleseed enriched by his service to others. The text of the speech flows on to its climax: . . . "In the name of the Commonwealth of Indiana, and in the name of this city of Fort Wayne, I dedicate . . . this *Johnny Appleseed Memorial Bridge.* . . .

The words roll out across the river. Johnny Appleseed, walking on the other side, lifts one hand and catches them adroitly. From force of old habit, he drops them into his story bag. He will take them back to Paradise and tell the children a new tale. They will look at him big-eyed, not certain whether to believe him, until finally he begins to twinkle and to grin. Then they will know it is just a folks' tale. Then they will laugh. So will he. For isn't it a thing beyond believing that a simple fellow like Johnny Appleseed should have a park and a bridge named for him, and in this old Miami town where, in spite of his own orchard acreage, he had been the humblest of all? Johnny chuckles.

A ray of afternoon sun shoots out from a rift in the clouds. For a moment the landscape shines as it should of a May day, the trees standing nymph-like in their delicate young green, the long sward of the park emerald, the river bright. Cars rush madly across the bridge, coming and going. Their speed and noise cause Johnny's pulse to beat faster than ever in old days, when he'd seen a wolf pack streaming after some prey. Hunching his shoulders so the noise won't jump down his spine, Johnny ducks beneath the bridge where the earth holds the supporting arch.

It is growing late. He must be getting on. He lifts his nose, sniffing. *Land o' mighty*, he'd give a pippin if he could take some apples to the children. It's not the time of year to find them hidden in the grass, or hanging from the bough, but surely he might smell them out in someone's root cellar—stored heaps of juicy *Rambos* and *Russets*, *Northern Spies* and *Fall Wines*. The golden apples of heaven—oh, they are as fair as flowers, with never a worm hole or a blemish on them! But the apples of earth—they have a wonderful tang to them, a tang of wildness descended from earth's first fruitage, and they have a mellowness born of deep earth-loam and nurtured by earth's blessed sun and rain. They have their flaws. They are not all of the same quality, but all have a quality that makes them a fruit of home, of merry and affectionate associations. The treasure of earth's apples! Something less than thought comes to Johnny, something rather odd and meaningless. Yet it has meaning for him, and for him alone. Years ago he had seen the shape of it, and heard the words of it, in childhood's fancy, perhaps, or in his dreams. *"Earth is an apple. Earth is a round apple,"* murmurs Johnny.

He plods through the sedges which grow along the river. He will meander over to Spy Run. Likely Captain Rudisill will have apples to spare. If not, Johnny may be obliged to follow the Maumee and its valley over into Ohio. He never did like to disappoint folks, and the children—well, even if he must travel a long way to find apples for them, he is used to walking.

Yea, though I walk through the valley—Yea, through the years of yesterday, and of today and of tomorrow—

THE END

ACKNOWLEDGMENTS

Fo r basic sources of information I wish to express my obligation to the following: Dr. Robert Price, head of the Department of English Literature at Otterbein College, foremost authority and compiler of *John Chapman, A Bibliography*, Swedenborg Press, 1944; to the centennial tribute entitled *Johnny Appleseed, A Voice in the Wilderness*, a pamphlet compiled by "his friends," 1945, containing the sketch map which appears in my book through the courtesy of the Swedenborg Press; to Robert C. Harris, of Fort Wayne, whose indefatigable search for historical evidence has resulted in the *Johnny Appleseed Source Book*, an impressive compilation of actual documents published as Vol. IX, Nos. 1–2, 1945, of *Old Fort News* under the auspices of the Allen County–Fort Wayne Historical Societies.

For making a great variety of material available to me I extend warm thanks to various librarians, particularly those of the Ohio and Indiana State Libraries, and the Mansfield and Fort Wayne Public Libraries. I also received aid from Florence E. Wheeler, former librarian of the Leominster, Massachusetts Public Library, and compiler of John Chapman's line of ancestors, accepted as definitive by Dr. Price.

The ballad fragments came from the *Henry Howe Historical Collections of Ohio*, Cincinnati, 1849; "The Boys of Ohio" and "Major Andrew's Execution" from Mary O. Eddy's *Ballads and Songs of Ohio*, J. J. Augustin, Inc., New York, 1939; "Follow Washington" and "Come Out, Ye Continentalers" from Edward A. Dolph's *Sound Off*, Rinehart and Company, New York, 1942.

Horticulturists and Swedenborgians furnished me with literature and advice. My thanks to the Reverend Klaas L. Peters, of the Swedenborgian Chapel of Indianapolis, for reading the manuscript. I treasure many happy recollections of favors granted and hospitality extended to me during my pilgrimage to various Ohio localities during the summer of 1948. Story Parade Inc. gave permission to include an adaptation of my own story "Seek-no-Further," originally published in the *Story Parade Magazine*, September, 1943.

Mabel Leigh Hunt
Indianapolis, Indiana
January, 1950

BOOKS BY MABEL LEIGH HUNT

For the Youngest

THE WONDERFUL BAKER

THE DOUBLE BIRTHDAY PRESENT

For the Middle Group

CRISTY AT SKIPPINGHILLS

STARS FOR CRISTY

MISS JELLYTOT'S VISIT

THE SIXTY-NINTH GRANDCHILD

MATILDA'S BUTTONS

YOUNG MAN-OF-THE-HOUSE

LITTLE GREY GOWN

BENJIE'S HAT

LITTLE GIRL WITH SEVEN NAMES

THE BOY WHO HAD NO BIRTHDAY

LUCINDA: *A Little Girl of 1860*

LADYCAKE FARM

For Older Boys and Girls

SINGING AMONG STRANGERS

BETTER KNOWN AS JOHNNY APPLESEED

"HAVE YOU SEEN TOM THUMB?"